Property Ladder

Design for Profit

CASSELL
ILLUSTRATED

Property Ladder

Design for Profit

SARAH BEENY

with
Jane Phillimore

First published in the United Kingdom in 2009
by Cassell Illustrated, a division of Octopus
Publishing Group Limited 2–4 Heron Quays,
London E14 4JP

Text by Sarah Beeny
with Jane Phillimore
Editorial, design and layouts by Essential Works
www.essentialworks.co.uk

ISBN 978 1 84403 645 5

A CIP catalogue for this book is available from the
British Library.

10 9 8 7 6 5 4 3 2 1

Printed and bound in China

Acknowledgements

A massive thank you to all those who work and who have worked with me over the years on *Property Ladder*. Thanks also to Jane Phillimore, Fiona Screen, Nina Sharman and Barbara Doherty at Essential Works, and to Mathew Clayton, Jo Wilson and Fiona Kellagher at Cassell. Also, thanks to Matt Sexton at B&Q superstores.

The publisher and author would particularly like to thank the following companies for supplying information and images to reproduce in this book:

Aestus Radiators – www.aestus-radiators.com
Ambience Bain (bathrooms) – www.ambiencebain.co.uk
Back to Front Exterior Design –
　　www.backtofrontexterior design.com
Boundary Bathrooms – www.boundarybathrooms.co.uk
Burton Constable Hall – www.burtonconstable.com
C. P. Hart (bathrooms) – www.cphart.co.uk
Camper & Nicholson – www.cnyachting.com
Carpet Base – 020 8675 2232
CC Concpts Ltd (original Circle® kitchen) –
　　www.compact-concepts.com
Clement Steel Windows – www.clementsteelwindows.com
Crucial Trading (floor coverings) – www.crucial-trading.com
Dalsouple (rubber flooring) – www.dalsouple.com
Evitavonni (bathrooms) – www.evitavonni.co.uk
Farrow & Ball (papers and paints) – www.farrow-ball.com
GlasSpace (Eagle SGW Ltd – glass structures) –
　　www.glasspace.com
Gordon Brown Roofing – www.gordonbrownroofing.co.uk

House Couturier (wallpapers) – www.housecouturier.com
John Cullen Lighting – www.johncullenlighting.co.uk
John Strand (hideaway kitchen) – www.johnstrand-mk.co.uk
London Basement Co Ltd – www.tlbc.co.uk
Myspace Garden Studios – www.myspacestudios.co.uk
Roger Oates (floors and fabrics) – www.rogeroates.com
Roger Wilde Ltd (specialist glass products) –
　　www.rogerwilde.com
Sanctuary Garden Offices – www.sanctuarygardenoffices.co.uk
Second Nature Kitchen Collection – www.sncollection.co.uk
Smith and Hale Construction – 01923 251883
Splash Distribution (bathrooms) – 01444 473355
Sunfold Systems (folding sliding doors) –
　　www.sunfoldsystems.co.uk
Talisman (lighting) – www.talismanlondon.com
Taylors Etc. (bathrooms) – www.taylorsetc.co.uk

Sarah's tried and recommended suppliers:

Amazing Grates – www.amazing-grates.com
Burton Constable Hall – www.burtonconstable.com
Camper & Nicholson – www.cnyachting.com
Carpet Base – 020 8675 2232
Clement Steel Windows – www.clementsteelwindows.com
Crucial Trading (floor coverings) – www.crucial-trading.com
Grants Blinds – www.grantsblinds.co.uk
Lightyourgarden.co.uk
Smith and Hale Construction – 01923 251883
Southern Staircases – www.southernstaircase.com
Sunfold Systems (folding sliding doors) –
　　www.sunfoldsystems.co.uk

Contents

Introduction

Introduction

There is a massive amount of nonsense written about design – long words, big concepts and a constant renaming of the wheel helps to keep good design just out of reach of much of the population. The reality, I believe, as with many things in life, is that good design is not actually that complicated and certainly not beyond the scope of anyone prepared to do a bit of research and think both creatively and logically.

Design covers both practicality and aesthetics. As a property is merely a vehicle for living, anything that makes that living easier from a practical point of view will understandably make it more valuable. Then there are aesthetics. It's true that a preoccupation with aesthetics can make for a good deal of unhappiness on many different levels, but aesthetics do nevertheless affect us, and cannot be ignored. Even those who claim they are unaffected will be made to smile just a little bit more by a beautiful piece of woodland with autumnal colours dripping all around them or the electric blue of the sky on a beautiful summer's day.

So, if you are producing a property that you actually want people to want to live in, then making the design really strong will undoubtedly mean that many buyers will set their heart on your creation.

I believe that good design can encompass and even embrace personal taste – there is no need for a bland white box with uninspiring detailing. Inject a little panache into things and, as long as the foundations are also right, your property will not only look great but also stand the test of time.

All fashion is cyclical and property is no exception. By looking at interiors that have stood the test of time, therefore, and then blending in a little of the new, you will automatically be on the right path.

Inside this book is a rich array of inspirational designs and images from different periods and styles. Your property may not be on quite as grand a scale as some of the homes in this book, but you can draw on these interiors as a resource to discover what looks good and works well together in any space. Get your detailing right and your property will be easier to live in and more inspiring to look at.

Front of House

Façades
Front Walls & Fences
Railings
Front Doors
Roofs
Front Gardens
Driveways

There are many random statistics about how many seconds it takes us to make up our minds about a person or place, but the underlying truth is that buyers decide whether they like a property very quickly indeed. So, without doubt, the first impressions of a house are very important. I believe that the way a house looks from the front is one of the most valuable selling tools around. What you don't want to do is to put off buyers before they actually reach the front door.

Fifty years ago, city society was very different from today; people took pride in washing their steps, polishing their brass letterboxes, even scrubbing their bit of pavement. Nowadays, though, it tends to only be the inside of our homes that we lavish 'tlc' on, abandoning the space beyond the front door as if it didn't exist. Even if it's not littered with bits of car engine, crisp packets or drink cans, it generally doesn't match up to the sparkling interiors within.

It need not take a great deal of money to make the front look cared for. Just picking the litter up is a start. Follow that with a lick of paint and bit of weeding and planting. If you have a communal front door, whether you're trying to sell or not, my theory is that it is often easier to scrub the common parts yourself than to argue with whoever's turn it is.

Of course, you can give a house a complete façade lift, changing the front door and windows, replacing dilapidated drainpipes and gutters, or even adding cladding. It's pricey, but it can often add substantial value to a plain or uninteresting property in a sought-after location. But whatever you do, remember the outside of a property remains a reflection of the inside. If you're selling, make sure it looks smart. The front of a house is a statement to the world about how you live.

Façades

In terms of square feet, most of a property's façade is made up of walls. Consequently, they have the greatest impact and it's worth making sure that the finish on walls is as good as it can be. Buyers will be put off by crumbling mortar, cracks in the stucco, or huge fissures in cladding, because they know they might find some real nasties beneath and that these problems may cost a pretty penny to fix. If brickwork needs repointing, render needs repairing or replacing, or the façade needs painting, I would always recommend that you do it before you put a property on the market.

RENDER & STUCCO

Traditionally, renders were applied to cover low-grade building materials such as porous brick or rubble stone as well as to protect walls from the elements. Renders come in many finishes from roughcast, which weathers well, to smooth. Stucco (an Italian term also known as pargeting in Suffolk) is a smooth flat finish popular in Georgian and Victorian times, often where lines are trowelled out of the render to give

Below: Render has been used for many centuries on both small and large properties.

Right: This unpromising 1950s property
(above) was transformed by a façade
makeover (below), carried out by
www.backtofrontexteriordesign.com

the impression of stone. Smooth renders, particularly stucco, can look fabulous but do need to be maintained. When repairing or re-rendering, most problems come when you mix old and new materials. Traditional lime-based renders are strong and flexible, allowing the walls to breathe and condensation to escape. Cement-based render is more common today. It is rigid and non-porous, so doesn't move or 'breathe' in the same way. On old buildings designed to allow for a little movement, this can make the render crack, allowing moisture in, which when frozen expands resulting in render falling off and the timber within to rot. More modern buildings will be constructed of these materials and so can be repaired with them with less risk. Check which products your builders are using before they start work.

There are also many synthetic renders with polymers, acrylics, aggregate reinforcements and anti-crack fibres which promise a low-maintenance, hermetically sealed finish on modern buildings. They come in a range of colours and textures.

PEBBLEDASH

Pebbledash is often considered to be very unappealing, but much of our inter-war housing stock is pebbledashed and it remains popular with homeowners because it is extremely durable and, on the whole, maintenance-free. Problems occur when it 'blows' – the thin top layer comes away from the base coat – or fissures appear which go through both layers. If you find pebbledash unappealing, this is a good time to remove it. However, it is as limpet-like as stone

DESIGNER NONSENSE

Don't be too afraid of colour on the outside of your house. Cream is not necessarily going to make it appealing – be a bit daring, but always consider the other properties in the street that your house stands next to.

Above: A part-rendered, and part-stuccoed early 19th-century property. **Below:** A contemporary rendered and timber-clad house.

cladding, so it means a time-consuming costly job that you'll find many builders reluctant to undertake.

STONE CLADDING

Stone cladding ranges from the bizarre to the splendid. We are all familiar with a Victorian terrace that has been 'stone cottaged' but larger and smoother sections of stone have been used for centuries with great effect. The trouble comes when trying to remove the cladding. The faces of the bricks are often damaged in the process so the façade may well need to be rendered and painted, or each brick face replaced with a new veneer – a bit like the process of capping teeth at a dentist. On the other hand, I think good modern stone cladding can transform a property from dreary to devastating. It's expensive, but stone is unique, durable, weathers well and is prestigious – a man's home originally being his stone-walled castle. If the design is sensitively chosen and you source local stone, it can look fabulous even on top of breeze blocks. On an unfashionable property in a good location, a stylish new cladding, be that stone or wood, could be the best investment you make.

TIMBER CLADDING

Wood has become more popular in recent years in the construction of houses in this country and a lot of newbuilds are now clad in wood or wood-effect. Timber-cladding can also be used on existing buildings, or on new parts of a builiding, even if the remainder of the building is brick. Weather-boarding gives an opportunity to insulate walls externally, lowering the risk of condensation, and protecting against severe weather conditions. Woods such as cedar are often used and look fabulous and, left untreated, weather to a lovely silvery-grey, although it's important to make sure the wood used is seasoned and pressure-treated to stop it warping. Personally I don't think UPVC wood-effect cladding ever looks like the real thing, but it's popular with some people because it's perceived as being maintenance-free. There is also a fibrous cement option which is more expensive than some timbers. Before you consider any form of cladding on an existing property, contact your local council to check whether planning permission is required, and find out from a structural engineer if your walls will hold the additional weight.

EXTERIOR PAINTING

If you're painting a façade in a terrace, look at the houses next door – yours doesn't have to match them, but it's better if it doesn't clash. Colours are affected by each other: you may think you are painting your house off-white, but if the property on one side is yellow and the other side stone, your off-white will look bright white. Always make sure that you buy the right kind of paint for your house: many modern exterior barrier paints are unsuitable for older rendered properties because the walls are unable to breathe.

Above: A good example of how strong bold colours can work fantastically well together.

Left: Coloured woodwork looks smart and full of personality. **Right:** Black is bold and modern.

Left: Contemporary eco-friendly housing in Manchester. **Right:** Stone and thatch cottage with hooded entrance.

Left: Mediterranean-style shutters give a bright, open feel. **Right:** Modern timber-clad property.

Left: Imposing ecclesiastical-style door. **Right:** Vibrantly painted façades brighten up a Victorian terrace.

Left: Boldly painted roughcast render on workers' cottages. **Right:** Grand Georgian façade with wisteria.

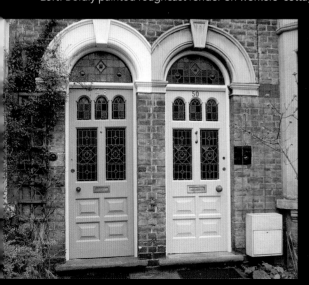

Front Walls & Fences

Should you put up a garden fence or a wall? Often it's a matter of cost. Fences are less expensive to install, but garden walls are more substantial, longer-lasting and define the border of the garden better. There are fences to suit every style of house, so don't restrict yourself to the usual slatted, panel and closeboard varieties. If you want to play it safe, a post and chain fence looks sophisticated outside a Georgian terrace; wrought-iron complements a Victorian façade; a traditional picket fence is perfect around a rose-covered cottage; and a utilitarian corrugated iron fence works brilliantly with a chic modern house.

Consistency is important so if your property is painted, think carefully before using a different colour for the fence or wall. With a brick house, make every effort to use the same type of brick and bonding for the front wall – you can find reclaimed bricks to match most types. With a stone property, build a stone wall from the same kind of stone. Before you build any fence or wall,

check with your local planning department. You will need planning permission if the structure is beside a highway and is over 1m in height. When you're designing a new front wall or fence, take the opportunity to find a place to store your rubbish bins or bikes, perhaps with a section high enough to hide them from view. But beware before you incorporate what you think is the perfect bin-sized container. Councils are prone to changing their minds about dustbin/wheelie bin sizes, so your well-crafted design might find itself in the bin.

Railings

Brick front walls in Victorian and Edwardian houses generally used to have metal railings on top of them, but many were removed during the Second World War, in theory to use as scrap metal. Putting them back is expensive and you're only likely to get your money back in the most gentrified areas of towns where housing costs are so high that spending a few thousand pounds extra on the look of a property can be added onto a sale price. You don't have to replace the original style but be aware that very *en vogue* designs are likely to date quickly, and traditional or classic contemporary railings will be likely to appeal to more people for longer.

GATES

A rusty, dilapidated front gate half-hanging off its hinges is unlikely to set anyone off on the right foot. On the other hand, a well-made, smoothly functioning gate gives a great first impression.

Below: The options for different detailing on wooden fencing are vast.

Opposite: Nothing looks more luscious on a townhouse than elaborate wrought-iron railings.

Front Doors

The front door is a great place to make a big statement. Bear in mind it's the only part of the house that people will stand and stare at very close up for several minutes at a time, so quality and finish are important. A badly painted front door with badly fitted door furniture is always a false economy. It smacks of a lack of attention to detail likely to be reflected inside. A nice, solid door is not only substantial but also better for security reasons and a reflection of what's to come inside. Never skimp on the quality of door furniture – but don't overdo it with knobs, knockers, bells and numbers all over the door. You're better off having fewer, good-quality pieces of door furniture. A simple but good-quality letterbox and bell gives a strong, positive impression. The paint colour you choose will depend on the style of your house and street, but be imaginative. Don't go for boring conformity. The front door is one area you can go to town on.

HOUSE NUMBERS

There are all sorts of weird and wonderful ways to display the name or number of your house but it's best to make it really clear if you want your post and deliveries to stand the best chance of arriving.

Below: Neutral colours do not have to be bland.

Left: A unique way of displaying a number. Right: A bold number '1' etched out of an opaque glass window.

Above (left, centre and right): Three classical front doors with traditional door furniture and house numbers.
Below left: A tiled, Spanish-inspired letterbox. Below right: Enamel French-style number plaque.

Above: A Georgian façade given a modern twist with horizontal bars on the windows.

Opposite: Doorways can be amusing and idiosyncratic as well as functional – this zany futuristic door pod raises a smile.

Left: Solar panels on modern houses. Right: Good salvaged slates and matching slates were used on this roof.

Left: Different-coloured tiled roofs. Centre: Ornate bargeboard over a dormer. Right: A decorative lead dome.
Below left: Decorative tiles on the roof of a tower. Below right: A tiled roof in need of replacement.

Roofs

Although they are high up, roofs are noticeable. If yours looks like it is at the end of its life, it can send alarm signals to potential buyers. It's one of the most expensive repairs a purchaser can be saddled with so it makes sense to make sure it's in good shape before putting a property on the market. Don't worry about scraping off moss or lichen. Some people think it looks unsightly but it doesn't actually damage the roof in any way. In fact, the cleaning process is more likely to cause roofing problems than leaving it well alone.

If you're selling a property 80 or more years old and the roof is showing signs of age, mortgage surveyors very often play safe and make useful comments, such as 'at some point this roof will need replacing'. Of course, this is true of every roof in the country but, written down in a survey, it may hold up the sale. Personally, I'd always reroof a tired roof in order to sell a property for a good price in a reasonable time, especially if you have nervous buyers.

ROOF WARNING SIGNS

1 Slipped, missing, cracked or broken slates or tiles: After a while nails rust and slates will tend to start slipping. You don't necessarily need a new roof as you can refit the fallen tiles/slates and hold in place with lead tingles/clips.
2 Worn lead flashing, soakers and valleys: These can wear thin and need replacing.
3 Worn pointing and flashing, especially around chimneys: This can be dangerous as the chimney will eventually collapse.
4 Sagging: This often occurs when slate is replaced with cheaper but heavier concrete or clay tiles and the original timbers are not strong enough to support them. The only solution to get the roof looking right again is to replace the whole structure including the timbers.

LEAKY ROOFS

Remember there is always a reason for a roof to be leaking as the water has to get in from somewhere. However, water may travel a distance from the source of water penetration to where it appears on the inside, and so solving a leak can be time-consuming and frustrating. Most slate and clay tile roofs leak very slightly anyway, but the water quickly evaporates. It only becomes a problem with very heavy downpours, where roof coverings are soaked for long periods of time and don't get chance to dry out. Most leaks occur because of cracked slates or tiles, or faults in the flashing. Once these have been located, they are relatively easy to repair. In most cases, there is no need to replace the whole roof.

DESIGNER REMINDERS

If clay or slate roof tiles are missing, try to match them with reclaimed ones. If you can't find an exact match, take tiles from a hidden part of the roof to fill the gap, then lay the closest match tiles in the hidden spot.

Hide white plastic meter boxes if you can. Brown or faux-brick ones blend in with brick walls. They can also be hidden with a timber-board cover, or in some cases semi-buried. Failing that, conceal with planting.

Door entry buzzer panels look neat and unobtrusive fitted flush with the stonework.

Front Gardens

If you're lucky enough to have some space at the front of your property, make the most of it. When designing a garden area, think of it essentially as a floor – the hard and soft landscaping of path, lawn or ground cover plants – with some vertical decorative touches such as a feature tree or wooden bench. A well-designed front garden should be simple and functional, and use materials that blend harmoniously with the surroundings. Get the path right first. Bricks, terracotta, stone and tiles look classic but you can choose any material, however unusual, that complements the style of your home. Traditional red or patterned tiles look

good leading up to the front door in a Victorian terrace, for example, whereas white and black gravel will complement a modern glass house.

A bit of greenery in the front garden softens the look of a property. Few of us have much time to look after our gardens, so low-maintenance planting is generally more attractive to buyers. Lawns, however tiny, need regular attention, so if your garden is small another option is to establish beds with low-growing, sculptural evergreens such as box or hebe, which don't need much care apart from occasional pruning.

Also consider planting against the house and using it as a backdrop. For instance, a climbing plant around the door, or bold,

Below: Simple, classic detailing enhances this terraced house.

colourful window boxes. Potted topiary creates a sculptural look and is a quick way of making your exterior appealing to a certain sort of buyer. In small front gardens, a single specimen tree makes an attractive focal point, although make sure that it is not one that sucks a lot of moisture from the ground which could affect the foundations.

Driveways

Many front gardens have been concreted over and turned into off-road parking spaces – in the north-east of England almost half the front gardens are now paved. Buyers, especially in inner city areas, like their own parking space, so having a paved offroad front drive may slightly increase the value of your home. But be aware that concrete stops water draining through the soil and so the property may be at risk of flash flooding from run-off rainwater. Whenever you're laying a new surface, whether it's a long driveway or small parking space, it's best to use porous paving and sub-base to allow the ground to absorb water. If you want to minimise environmental impact, pave over the smallest area you can.

THAT LITTLE BIT EXTRA...

Fabulous garden lighting is the ultimate luxury. Many people have blazing security lights in their front garden so something subtle, perhaps underlighting feature plants or backlighting, or even set into a path, is a big treat. With a remote control box, you can change the light settings and display throughout the year. Contact a company that specialises in garden lighting design.

Above: An inspirational front garden! Clipped yews and urns line the path to Belton House. **Below:** Subtle lighting can be used to draw the eye towards a property.

Eating

Our eating habits have changed enormously over the past 50 years. Time is now a valuable commodity and so preparation time for meals has become a dirty word. The way we use our eating areas has changed too. Kitchens are no longer small, dark, functional rooms with a sink, a stove, a few drawers and a table. Today they are light, airy, informal spaces with sleek wall-to-floor storage, big fridges, ranges, microwaves, and many implements and appliances. They tend to be the heart of a house, where everyone gets together to chat and chill out as well as eat and cook. Often, they're the most glamorous room, too, with cathedral-beamed ceilings, cavernous space and walls of glass bringing the outside in.

Of course, this is not always achievable. At the other end of the spectrum, many people don't have a table and chairs and eat all their meals on the sofa in front of the television. Which is fine if you're a student or carefree couple, but less good for everyone else. Studies show that children benefit from eating at least four telly-free meals a week with their family. They have lower rates of obesity, fewer eating disorders, better exam results and less depression. So perhaps, surprisingly, a well-organised kitchen brings psychological as well as practical benefits.

However, there's no point having a spanking kitchen if you've got a dodgy roof and leaky plumbing. But if your kitchen is dark and pokey it is unlikely to help sell your house. Think carefully about your options. Build sideways or backwards. Rethink your light sources and storage. Simple changes can make a big difference. Saint Jamie Oliver has made it cool for men to be creative about cooking so now pretty much every buyer, male or female, will be looking for a well-functioning kitchen area. It's a good idea to make sure you've got one, whatever the size of your home.

Galley Kitchens

Just because a kitchen is small, it doesn't mean it can't be fabulous. The term 'galley kitchen' comes from the narrow cooking corridors on barges and boats, where efficient use of very limited space and facilities was essential. Today, creating a galley is easier than ever before, because high-tech appliances and integrated units mean that you can literally fit a kitchen into a corner.

When you're compromised on space, there are two ways to go: hide everything away behind a sleek facade so the kitchen merges seamlessly into the living area. Or make the kitchen a feature, with everything on display. There may only be room for a sleek breakfast bar worktop area with a couple of high stools. If you enjoy cooking, you might want to have pots and pans hanging down and handy. Or, if you like entertaining, hide the galley behind sliding doors which you throw open when guests arrive, so you can chat while you cook. Flexibility is key and props like foldable, stackable tables and chairs make the very best use of space.

If you're on a tight budget, cheaper white appliances and units merge visually into one. It costs more to buy and build in fully integrated appliances, but it's easier on the eye. If money is no object then a composite work surface – with an integrated sink – looks very stylish.

There is no rule about the colour you paint your galley, or whether it blends in or stands out from the rest of your living area. But in a small space, bear in mind that people have to stand closer to everything, so a poor finish is more noticable.

GREAT SPACE SAVERS

For **clutter-free worktops**, hide your countertop appliances in a cupboard at worktop height with lots of sockets inside and a vertical sliding door. Pull them out for use, ready plugged in, only when you need them.
Three-way combination microwaves come with fan oven and grill so are hugely practical for galley kitchens.
For **draining**, invest in an over-the-sink draining cupboard so crockery and pots drip can dry out of sight.
Slimline dishwashers are only 450mm wide.

Studio Kitchens

All-in-one kitchens work well in tiny studio spaces. There are some really clever concepts around, such as 180-degree revolving kitchens (see opposite, above right) with an integrated sink, fridge, dishwasher, microwave and hob, storage and a tiny eating area, all in less than 1.8m space. Or a built-in hideway kitchen (see opposite, below right), where you open sleek cupboards to reveal all. Otherwise go for small appliances that you can bring out or hide away: you can get tabletop ovens and washing machines, and a dishwasher that fits in a drawer.

Above: A very smart galley on a boat. Above right: The fully fitted 180 degree, revolving kitchen.
Below: Bright reflecting surfaces make a galley look bigger. Below right: A kitchen-in-a-cupboard.

DESIGNER NONSENSE

Kitchen specialists always talk about the ergonomic 'work triangle' – apparently, the total distance between the fridge, hob and sink must be between 3.5m to 8m (12ft to 26ft), with minimal household traffic through the area. It's meant to make kitchen use easier, but it's always seemed a load of designer nonsense to me.

Kitchen/Breakfast Rooms

When there are young children around, preparing, feeding and cleaning up after a family takes up much of the day. Even with older children, time is often so short that preparation for a meal is frequently done in conjunction with eating it. So most families love eating in the kitchen, and the priority if you're selling a family house is to have a kitchen/breakfast room large enough for a good table and chairs. If it isn't, think about extending sideways or into the garden, or lose another room – usually the old 'back' dining room in Victorian houses – to increase the square footage.

Above: Dark wooden flooring, pale walls and an Aga – a classic and welcoming look.

Right: Folding doors let in maximum light and bring the garden into the house. **Below right:** A freestanding dresser provides useful storage.

Most people want to open their kitchen doors wide on a sunny day and let the outside in. If possible, put in glazed double doors leading to the garden so you get the benefit of great views even in the depths of winter. The kitchen/breakfast room has two functions: cooking and eating. I'd always place the eating zone near the French doors where there's good natural light. The kitchen zone can afford to be in the darker part of the room as you generally cook under artificial light. In a long rectangular space, it's best to try to run kitchen units halfway down both sides, rather than all the way down only one wall, because, ideally both areas can then be used independently. If you find that you're short on storage, it's better to put a free-standing dresser in the eating area.

Although it has two functions this is still one room, and it's important to think of the design as a whole. You don't want a traditional pine-topped table alongside dark Iroko wood kitchen cabinets. Yet it's a fallacy that you have to have the same flooring throughout. Different flooring can actually make the space feel bigger.

Finally, the one thing many people forget about is a dedicated bin and recycling area. In an ideal world, you'd hide all the rubbish out of sight inside an integrated unit, with three or more sections for different types of waste. But if it's too late for that, stylish stand-alone bins look good and you can get non-touch sensor versions which open automatically.

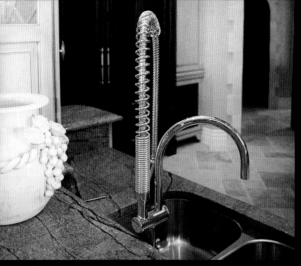

Left: A single-lever mixer tap with a useful handspray facility. **Right**: A slim, pull-out shelf perfect for a laptop.

Left: Handy scales built into the worktop. **Right**: A stainless steel draught beer dispenser for chilled pints.

Left: Boiling water taps are becoming popular. **Right**: A little luxury – a cappacino maker fitted into kitchen units.

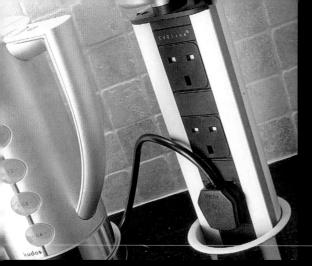

Left: A high-rise power point means an end to multiple wall sockets. **Right**: Hideaway ironing board.

Left: Built-in undershelf spotlights illuminate work surfaces. **Right**: A tiny sink, useful for peeling vegetables.

Left: Sinks come in all shapes and sizes! **Right**: A streamlined hood over a stone hob – easy to keep clean.

Kitchen/Living Rooms

Most people today want relaxed and informal living spaces and, as a result, the open-plan family kitchen/living room has become extremely popular. Although one big room, it has three different zones for cooking, eating and living. In concept it's very similar to a studio flat with kitchen, table and sofa. Just a lot bigger. Space is the vital element here: you need square footage to make it work, and often in a family house a whole basement is given over to it. This living arrangement is very desirable for families and works extremely well provided there is at least one separate reception room where people can escape the communal space.

Outside access is also key as you need to be able to fully appreciate and benefit from an upturn in our weather fortunes. If you can have a back door cloakroom and loo right next to this room it's a bonus.

There should be consistency between the three zones – so if you want a contemporary style, you're looking to make the whole lot contemporary. However, think about using different but complementary flooring and lighting to designate different zones. You need bright, focused lights in the kitchen zone, and a softer, more diffuse glow in the eating and living areas.

Ideally, the living area should feel cosy and warm. But big family kitchens – even ones with oven and Aga heat – can feel cold, especially if there is a large external glass area. I'd always put a fireplace in the living area, if you can, as it makes a good focal point as well as an economical heat source. Welcoming, comfortable and hard-wearing sofas are essential, and you'll probably want a television – making life easier for informal viewing.

THAT LITTLE BIT EXTRA...

The ultimate luxury in an open plan kitchen/living room is a wood burner. Traditional or modern, they are heat- and energy-efficient and also very safe – a big advantage in a family room. Leave them lit when you go up to bed – just shut the front panel door first.

Left: A well-designed, contemporary three-zone living room with focused lighting in the dining and kitchen areas.

Above: Brick, wood and lots of light in this open-plan loft. **Above right:** Dark floors, furniture and glazing bars provide design consistency. **Below:** The chic, glossy eating zone contrasts with the textures in the cosy living area.

Split-Level Kitchens

In large areas with cavernous high ceilings, where there is a shortage of light, split-level kitchens are a great solution as they make a big space appear inviting and cosy. The mezzanine level can be raised to whatever the height allows and suits the area – sometimes a couple of steps is enough to make a difference visually; sometimes you might need a short flight of stairs, perhaps curving around a corner.

Stairs are expensive to install so I would generally avoid the latest fashion and go instead for classic good looks that will stand the test of time. In a kitchen, safety is an issue, so choose a slip-free surface with low risers and deep treads. The key to a successful split-level kitchen is to make the two zones work well together. It doesn't particularly matter which way round you arrange the kitchen and diner but you want to avoid a top-heavy look, so don't put floor-to-ceiling units on the upper area. Bear in mind, too, that you mostly stand in the kitchen, and sit in the dining area, so if you want to chat to friends while cooking, the kitchen is better on the lower level. Heat rises, so this arrangement will also be more energy-efficient. It's a good idea to try and minimise household traffic through the dining area to make it a quiet and cosy spot.

Below: The smart use of symmetry makes this kitchen a practical as well as beautiful space.

Above: A small, galley mezzanine-level kitchen feels spacious because of the graceful curves of the double-height ceiling. The eating area is below.

The biggest problem with split-level kitchens is a lack of worktops and storage in the kitchen area. There is simply less wall space. Most split–levels have a mid-height structure between the two zones which you can utilise on the kitchen side by running work surfaces and below-waist storage along it. Pull-out storage or even larder space can be added under the mezzanine provided you have safe side access.

Noise and smells float through split-level kitchens, so use soft furnishings to absorb sound and install good extraction. I would always make sure that lighting for the two areas is independent and can be controlled from both lower and upper floors.

Storage

Now kitchens have become the nerve centre of the house, clever storage solutions make the most of every inch of space. It's worth every penny – sufficient and efficient storage will always add value.

Smart and streamlined dedicated drawers for a selection of knives and utensils.

Corner pull-outs are especially useful, bringing what's on the shelves out to you.

Baskets in wood, metal or wicker are generally associated with more traditional-style kitchens.

Wooden drainers are hard to maintain but are an economic way of achieving a top-end look.

Swing-out larders such as this one make excellent use of kitchen space.

Hide tea towels and other cleaning clutter out of sight inside a slimline pull-out cupboard.

A butcher's trolley gives an extra work surface and shelves, and can be wheeled out of the way.

Waste sorting base unit – a recycling solution to aid the ever-growing issues arising from kitchen waste.

Dining Rooms

With every square foot of a property costing a premium and lifestyles becoming less and less formal, the dining room is often the first room to be sacrificed. So today the dining room is, generally, a luxury found only in top-end homes because it needs to come as well as, rather than instead of, a good-sized kitchen/breakfast room.

In reality, there are many good reasons to separate cooking and eating areas, not least to prevent cooking smells, steam and the noise of crashing pots permeating the living area. But dining rooms are generally used only in the evenings, or on special occasions, so a separate dining room is certainly a luxury.

In terms of design, this is one room where you can afford to get a little carried away. Dining rooms should be cosy spaces, and are often painted in warm, dark shades of red or green. They are used mostly in the evenings, so light is less important – therefore, a dark, north-facing room is ideal. Personally I'd always pop in a serving hatch through to the kitchen if you possibly can, even though many people feel they are a 1970s joke. Once you've had one, you'll never want to live without it.

Acoustics are a crucial factor in an area where people are chatting and socialising, so you really need fabrics and soft furnishings – curtains, carpets, even wallpaper – to absorb the noise. Although they are becoming extinct, you may want to consider smokers and fit extraction, if you don't want to send people out into the cold.

Opposite: A period-style dining room with warm colours looks welcoming by candlelight.

MULTI-PURPOSE DINING ROOMS

A dining room is one room that is rarely used so make it a dual-function room. Use it as an occasional office, organised so that you can hide papers and computers in cupboards when you eat. If you have older children, a dining room is a good quiet homework area. Or make it into a games room. A large dining table can double as a table tennis arena or you can buy substantial wooden billiard/dining tables with leaves that either spin over or lift off to reveal a billiard/pool table below. They come dual-height so you can lower them for eating, and raise them for playing.

Below: In this traditional dining room, contrasting patterns and fabrics work well.

Utility Rooms

Few homes now have a dedicated room for laundry, clothes-drying and to store the mop and vacuum cleaner. Instead, now that space carries such a premium in price, the washing machine is in the kitchen and we dry clothes in the dryer – or on radiators throughout the house. Wanting larger kitchens has been the kiss of death to the laundry/utility room, but they still very much have their place. If you've got a utility room, you will consider yourself very lucky. If you haven't, don't dismiss the possibility of clawing back some space to create one. It might feel like a waste but it actually frees up your living space and makes it more efficient to live in; consequently, it's a huge selling point in a family house.

Ideally, a utility area houses the washing machine, dryer, ironing board, a sink and drying pulley. It also has storage space for

cleaning utensils, mops, vacuums, vases and other household necessaries, well away from the food preparation areas. It doesn't need to have great head height or be beautifully finished – an unconverted basement is a good location as long as it's not too damp and you provide good ventilation. You won't regret it. This is the engine room that keeps the rest of a house running smoothly and tidily, and if you have the space it's well worth creating one.

Larders

The first casualty of refrigerators back in the 1950s was the larder. But actually there are a whole range of foods – bread, eggs, cakes, cereals, cheese, jams, pickles, cooked meats, beer and most vegetables – which benefit from being in a cool rather than cold atmosphere, and currently reside in the fridge or too-warm cupboards in the kitchen. If you're a serious cook or have a large family, a walk-in larder is the greatest luxury you can imagine.

A larder needs to be dark and cool, with good ventilation, best achieved with a stone floor and a small, wire-mesh window to stop flies getting in while providing ventilation. Situate it along an outside wall, and plan lots of open shelves – marble or stone were traditionally used to keep food cool – above worktop surface height.This is a utilitarian space, so pack it with storage. There should be space to house crockery, utensils and pots and pans, leaving your kitchen less cluttered. A larder is not for everyone but, in the right house, it's an absolute winner.

Left: A dedicated laundry/utility room frees up living space.

Above: A corner of the larder at Petworth House, with various storage containers, jugs and a set of scales.

DESIGNER REMINDERS

In a cellar, you'll need to sort out drainage for a utility room. If the outlet at the bottom of the existing manhole is higher than the cellar floor, you'll have to pump waste water up to it.

If size makes a dedicated utility room impossible, think about putting the washing machine/dryer into a bathroom cupboard, continental-style. It frees up kitchen space.

Bathing

Bathrooms, chic, luxurious and in plentiful supply, are a modern day phenomenon. A century or so ago, loos were outside closets and the weekly bath in the average Victorian terrace was taken in a tin tub in front of the kitchen range. In 1951, 40 per cent of houses in Britain had no fixed bath and even in 1963 Harold Wilson was lamenting that 15 million Britons lived in homes without a plumbed-in bath. Now in that same Victorian terraced house there will be at least one bathroom and if you don't bathe once or even twice a day, people consider you to be positively unclean.

We've come a long way. Bathrooms are now expected to be simple, well-designed, luxurious and calm – and plentiful. No longer can a five-bedroomed house have a single bathroom. Luxury developments come with an en suite for every bedroom and, in future, I suspect this will be pretty commonplace for all new homes. But think carefully before you pinch space from bedrooms or hallways to create small en suites. Houses are all about balance, and I believe that a good working ratio for how we live today is at least one bathroom for three bedrooms, with a second loo as backup. If you've got space, you would also ideally create an en suite for the master bedroom.

The bathroom is the one room in the house which can afford to give up light and space, so small, windowless bathrooms are a reasonable compromise. Although, even in the tiniest space, you can create a well-designed and relaxing sanctuary from the stresses of the day. We spend a lot on our bathrooms – more than £1 billion a year on fittings and fixtures – but think twice before buying the very latest trendsetting bath or spa unit unless you have a very top-end development. Instead, go for a look of simple luxury.

Bathroom Design

The key to creating bathroom luxury, whatever your market and budget, is to keep the look clean and simple. Make a scale drawing of the room and play around with the various positions of the bath, shower, loo and basin. Beware of non-matching sanitaryware because, even if all the fittings are white, the shades can vary dramatically. While they can be impractical, corner and offset baths can sometimes make good use of space and, remember, you can choose where to position the taps. In a room too small for a separate shower, you can still create a good showering experience by fitting a good-quality shower door to the bath. Ideally every bath needs a bath/shower mixer with a hose attachment to clean it and for washing hair.

A bathroom is one area where you can really release your design dreams but, if you're planning on ever selling, the key is in the execution. A poor finish will always let you down. Sleek, modern fittings can work well even in a feature-filled Victorian or Edwardian house. The main family bathroom has different requirements from secondary bathrooms. It needs practicality and space above all else.

Coloured bathroom suites were popular a few decades ago, and I'll put money on it that they'll be right back in fashion before we know it, though perhaps not quite yet. Other colours used in bathrooms have to work with the colour of the sanitaryware – natural tones and natural materials such as stone, slate, marble and wood will tend to stand the test of fashion time.

Opposite: Using similar colourwash on the walls, bath panels and floor gives a shabby-chic style.
Below: Bold, low-level horizontal stripes of red and black ground this modern bathroom.

DESIGNER BATHTUBS

When budget allows, consider using a statement bathtub such as a free-standing spoon bath, wood or glass tub. But remember, designer bathtubs come with a caveat. Many are not actually that practical. Some have straight sides and a flat bottom, like a swimming pool, so you can't lie down in them. Or they're extravagantly curved and take up acres of space. They're great fun when you want a luxury hotel environment, but think carefully before fitting one. It's unlikely to add as much value as it costs, so it's only worth it if you'll get sufficient enjoyment from it yourself while you're there.

VICTORIAN ROLL-TOPS

Roll-top baths can look gorgeous – which is why we all love the Flake adverts – but they're not tremendously easy to live with on a daily basis. There's nowhere to put your soap, shampoo, flannel and other bath essentials apart from plonking them on a table beside the bath, or using an old-fashioned bath rack across your knees. One solution is to build a little hole or shelf in the wall beside the bath, where you can store your bottles out of the way but within easy arm's reach for when you're dripping wet and reaching for the soap or shampoo.

EN SUITES

An en suite is fast becoming a must-have for the master bedroom. In designer chic properties it's quite common to lose the 'en' and have an open-plan bathing area within the bedroom. There's something luxurious about having a bath in your bedroom – though there's an irony in the fact that it's a return to the days when you wallowed in a tin tub in front of the bedroom fire. But I personally really think you should draw the line at open-plan loos.

Above: A modern egg-shaped bath can look good in an open-plan en suite. **Opposite:** Freestanding baths – quirky luxury (above) or traditional roll-top with wooden lip (below).

DESIGNER REMINDERS

I'd be wary of substituting a shower for a bath in a one-bathroom property, though stand-alone shower rooms work well as a second bathroom option.

When choosing an extractor fan, go for the quietest one. You don't want to hear it whirring away while you're trying to sleep next door.

Beware of badly made reproduction roll-tops – they look cheap and tacky.

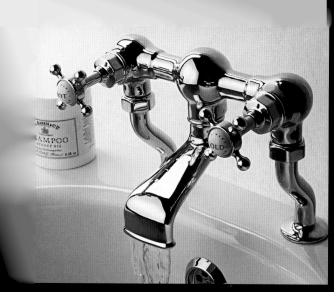

Left: Traditional Victorian-style mixer tap. **Right:** Bath concealed in a Jacobean-style cupboard.

Left: An imposing slipper clawfoot tub. **Right:** A contemporary mixer tap over a stone black basin.

Left: His 'n' hers countertop basins. **Right:** Black, white and grey are a great combination in this bathroom.

Left: Discreet underbasin storage. **Right:** A curvy sensuous bathtub with standing taps to match.

Left: A smooth-cornered bath creates a sgtrong designed look. **Right:** A copper and zinc statement bathtub.

Left: Slick, super-streamlined taps. **Right:** Corner sinks make good use of space in tiny bathrooms.

Above: A distressed, 'unfinished' look with a bare bulb fitting may not be for everyone but is a strong statement.

Opposite: Quirky and comfortable, this attic bathroom-in-a-corridor has bags of personality and shows great use of space.

Showers

Personally, I hate showers – in fact, if I was prime minister I'd probably make the things illegal. However, I accept that most people find that the shower is the perfect way to kickstart the day – so in a house that you're going to sell they are a necessary evil! Shower enclosure design is becoming simpler, less cluttered and easier to keep clean, with walk-in options, curved glass panels and low-level trays. As a result, you can make a great design statement with a shower.

Shower areas are usually tight on space, therefore you want to make use of every millimetre you've got. Many enclosures come in flexible sizes from 700mm to 1200mm or more, with offset doors so you can slot them into corners. Even curved enclosures come with sliding or hinged doors. Walk-in showers, with a 'dry' area at one end where you can hang towels and robes, are another option, although they take up almost as much room as a bath. If you're lucky enough to have the space, minimalist walk-in glass panels supported by overhead wall braces are very appealing to the luxury end of the market.

POWER SHOWERS

It's a myth that showers use less water than baths, at least when you're talking about modern power showers. They are phenomenally expensive to fit and environmentally quite appalling. In five minutes under a power shower, you use about 120 litres of water, which is enough

Above: Simple, uncluttered showering.
Left: A modern all-over body shower contrasts with a retro-style brick enclosure.

to fill a whole bath. By contrast, ordinary showers use around 35 litres of water. However, if you feel that a power shower is essential, then you'll generally need to fit a pump to the shower's water supply. Combination boilers that heat water as it is used will not be suitable, so check with your plumber.

Below: Using the same tiles on the walls and floors will give a bathroom an authentic wet room feel. Here the inner side of the door has been tiled to create a luxurious shower hideaway.

DOWNSTAIRS SHOWERS

Traditionally, a downstairs shower is the spider pit, with a plastic shower curtain that sticks to you and freeze-making lino on the floor. Downstairs showers are good value in a house near a beach or in the countryside as a place to hose down wetsuits or wash mud off. But if it's not that kind of property, walking downstairs to shower in a tiny room off the kitchen is not pleasant. Provided you have an upstairs bathroom, I suggest remodelling the area as a loo, separate utility space, or making it part of a kitchen.

SHOWERHEADS AND FITTINGS

Do you need a hydro-massage column or all-over body jets in your shower, or will a simple fixed-head attachment do? The only must for a luxurious-feeling bathroom is a high-level showerhead. That doesn't necessarily mean a fixed overhead shower. They look fantastic but can be difficult to live with as getting your hair wet is unavoidable, and it's hard to clean out the shower enclosure afterwards. If you go for a fixed overhead, even a flexible one, I'd suggest installing a handset shower as well.

VENTILATION

Showers, and especially power showers, produce massive quantities of steam so getting the ventilation right is crucial to keeping your shower room looking good. Go for the biggest and most effective option you can afford. Extractor fans can be sited through an external wall or through a duct at a high level in the room. For maximum effect, the fan should be placed at the other side of the room from the main air source.

Left: A sleek shower panel in a wet room can be a work of art in its own right.

WET ROOMS

Wet rooms are often beautiful but sometimes they can be less than practical. As the name suggests, everything gets wet, so you end up with a wet loo seat, wet loo rolls, wet sink, wet towels. They work brilliantly in hot countries where water evaporates fast, but in Britain you need to understand their limitations, and think carefully before you install one.

Wet rooms effectively turn the whole room into a shower area, with the floor area tiled on a slight slope so that water runs into the drain. Any leak can do serious damage to the floor below. Despite this, I think wet rooms definitely have a place. They can transform a small shower area into an amazing cleaning experience, giving your property that all-important selling point.

DESIGNER NONSENSE

In bachelor designer developments, bathrooms often come with plasma television screens. Personally, I think this is taking gadgetry one step too far. Surely the natural, simple tranquillity of bathing would be horribly interrupted by having a television in the bathroom.

People warn against wooden floors in bathrooms, but they can look fabulous and are workable provided you choose a resilient hardwood, such as oak or ash, and use a suitable, durable coating. To slow down wear and tear, make sure ventilation is good and clear up water spills before leaving the room.

LOOS

Toilet, loo, lavatory, dunny, ladies' room, bog, WC, or whatever you call it, in a family house, a ground-floor loo is essential. Yet it is often a dark, damp, depressing little space – the room that time forgot. I think downstairs loos need jollying up. Have a bit of a laugh with it. If you've got some outrageous wallpaper or a wild paint colour mulling around your head, try it out. As ever, make it luxurious by getting the pipework out of sight, then think about creating a welcoming space that makes people smile inside.

THE BEST LOOS

The Victorians built many of our sewage systems; they really embraced the loo and had fabulous ones, with big, luxuriously comfy wooden seats that aren't cold to the touch. If you've got a small room, there are great space-saving loos which slot into corners, and many manufacturers have cloakroom ranges with sized-down hand basins and taps to match.

Wall-hung pans look neat and discreet, and self-closing seats are a good idea. The high-tech Japanese even have a bidet-cum-loo which squirts water 'where you need it' and then blow-dries you too – although this may be a little scary for most Brits.

Left (above): An unusual wooden cistern with a porcelain pan in a cosy cloakroom.
Left (below): Mixing traditional wooden panelling with modern toilet fittings.
Opposite: The basin and wooden seated toilet (thunderbox) at the National Trust's Plas Newydd, on the Isle of Anglesey, Wales.

Statement Bathrooms

The ultimate luxury is to have a completely over-the-top bathing experience in a beautifully designed bathroom. You might dream of creating a Roman bath-house with wall mosaics, an opulent wood and brass Victorian bathroom or a Moroccan palace effect. I have one word of advice here: once you've started, don't get cold feet – just go for it! Yes, these creations are a little impractical and will only appeal to a limited market. But, in the right house, they will truly fire the imagination of anyone who likes to indulge their eccentric side like yourself.

Eco Bathrooms

There's a lot we can do to make our homes more eco-friendly, and a lot of it can be done in the bathroom. We're each using 70 per cent more water than we did 30 years ago, which is a pretty stark statistic. Just flushing the loo accounts for about 30 per cent of water usage today. Making the endless bathrooms we do have less wasteful is something that's on everyone's minds. It makes good developer sense, too, as people think more about their water bills. Old loos use 9 or 10 litres of water at a time, whereas new dual-flush cisterns use about 6 litres on full flush and 4 litres on short flush – and you can get ultra-efficient loos that short-flush with about 2 litres of water.

A little water-saving action can make a big difference in the bathroom. It's easy to fit aerator taps and low-flow showerheads, which restrict the flow of water without reducing water pressure. Going the whole distance and recycling 'grey' waste bathroom water demands large water storage areas and careful handling to keep it well away from the mains supply, so it is necessarily complicated. But technology is coming on in leaps and bounds in this area and I'm pretty sure there will be a lot more green options for the bathroom in the near future so keep up to date with developments.

THAT LITTLE BIT EXTRA...

If you can make it work, fit a laundry chute in the bathroom. It is a fantastic feature and a great timesaver for people with busy lives. There's an old-world glamour to chucking all your laundry into the bathroom chute, even if you have to sort it yourself at the other end!

You need free space between the floors without plumbing, wires or other obstructions. You can hide the chute ends in cupboards, with a big laundry basket at the bottom. Perhaps this is a little impractical for the majority of homes!

Above: Once you have started down a route, go for it! This Moroccan bathroom has a powerful feel.

Windows

Windows in a house are like eyes on a face. If they're too big or small it can throw all other details out of kilter, but get them in proportion and the whole will, generally, be considered beautiful. The important thing is not to create window features that stand out individually, but that work with the rest of the house. As a general rule, however, I think it's better to put in larger rather than smaller windows, because in this country we all crave natural light.

A window is essentially a hole in the wall with a lintel above which keeps the wall standing. It's expensive to move these holes, and can have a dramatic effect on the look of the property, so think carefully and check planning regulations before you start.

If you're replacing window frames, you have three options: wood, UPVC (Unplasticised Polyvinyl Chloride) or metal – usually aluminium or steel. Be cautious about fitting UVPC windows. They're sold as zero-maintenance, which is true for their short lifespan, after which they will need entirely replacing. Also, they can be clumsy in design and look inappropriate in an older property. Wooden windows, however, properly maintained, last indefinitely and are far more environmentally sound. The safest thing is to stick with the type of windows that would originally have been in the house. In Victorian and Edwardian properties, this means wooden sashes. In 1930s and 1940s houses, elegant metal frames with fine glazing bars. Putting Elizabethan-style lead criss-cross casements into a Victorian house will just look bizarre.

In a window, which is ultimately a bit of surround with glass in the middle, it's the details that count if you want to add value, style and authenticity to your property. My advice is to shop carefully for your windows. They will make or break your property.

Short History of Windows...

Originally we had the simple yet extremely functional arrow slit, followed by tiny 'wind eyes' that let smoke out and air in...

In the 15th and 16th centuries windows got bigger, with square and diamond-shaped lights with leaded strips...

Sash windows were introduced in the 17th century, and tall, small-paned Georgian windows with rounded arches arrived...

The Victorians liked bigger windowpanes in their bays and bows...

Edwardians went for coloured glass and fancy detailing...

Between the wars, metal-framed windows changed the look of our houses...

But condensation was a problem. So in the 1960s and 1970s, we returned to wooden frames for our big picture windows…

In the 1980s, anything went, including UPVC. In the 1990s, suburban 'Tudorbethan' made use of plastic and vinyl frames…

And today's high-performance glass means we have light-filled houses with see-through walls and roofs as well as windows…

BRIEF WINDOW GLOSSARY

Awning: top-hung pivot window, opening out from the bottom of the frame.

Bow or bay: a window with a central and two flanker units projecting from the wall of the house to form an alcove. They can be sash, casement or awning windows.

Casement: a hinged window which opens outwards like a door.

Double-glazed: two sheets of glass with air or gas between that create an insulating barrier to reduce heat loss and improve energy efficiency. Modern sealed units can be fitted to existing windows.

Glazing bar: the supporting or dividing structure in a window. Can be made of wood, metal or synthetics.

Lights: windowpanes or glass divisions within a window.

Oriel: a projecting window, usually on upper floors, supported by brackets.

Picture window: large expanse of non-opening glass in a window frame.

Quarries: small square or diamonds of glass, often set into lead strips to give leaded lights.

Sash: a window with two sashes placed one above the other, sliding in different grooves on a frame. With single-hung sashes, the top sash is fixed and stationary; with double-hung sashes both parts move up and down.

Sliding: windows that open by sliding horizontally across a frame.

Transom: a small window above a window or door. Ornamental in design, they give extra light. Opening transoms allow rising warm air to escape.

Feature Windows

Think long and hard before adding a feature window without considering whether it fits in with the rest of the property. Round, arched, Gothic, geometric or oval feature windows look fantastically effective in the right place and period of house but appalling if you don't get it exactly right. If in any doubt, do some hard research or get an architect to help you.

ROOF WINDOWS

Rooflights and lantern lights – the pyramid-shaped glass structures you find on flat roofs – are a great way to bring light into the room below and can be a dramatic feature in themselves. If you're converting a loft space, rooflights increase natural light without altering the roof line, and dormer windows or a mansard roof will give greater headroom and walkabout area. In dark stairwells, a sun tunnel in the roof will allow natural light to flood down and transform the area below and are relatively inexpensive.

FLOOR WINDOWS

People nowadays want light-filled rooms throughout. Advances in glass technology mean that you can build reinforced glass sections into floors to let light flow vertically through the house. Dark basements can be transformed by putting in a well-designed 'floor window' of toughened, walk-on glass through the ceiling into the room above – make it opaque if you're worried about privacy. In roof gardens, putting in small areas of anti-slip pedestrianised glass will bring bright sunlight to the room below without losing useful outdoor space.

Building with Glass

A glass feature wall or light-bringing retractable glass roof can be sensational and a massive selling point of a house. But glass – even double- and triple-glazed – gives a poor thermal performance compared to other building materials. New building regulations (2006, Part L, see www.planningportal.gov.uk for details) mean that you have to assess the total thermal efficiency of your property before making changes. To get planning permission for a glass façade or roof, you'll have to compensate by improving thermal performance and energy efficiency elsewhere in the house, perhaps by insulating walls or the roof, or adding solar panels. These thermal-offset calculations are complex, so contact your local council planning department or ask an architect for advice.

Above: A semi-circular window adds drama.
Opposite: A chic, light-filled family house with glazed walls and ceiling.

Left: Traditional stone window mullions and ledges. **Right:** Dormer windows bring light and space into roofs.

Left: Daylight streams through a wall of French doors. **Right:** Windows become walls in a contemporary house.

Left: A traditional Edwardian bay with wooden sashes. **Right:** Georgian-inspired floor-to-ceiling French windows.

Left: Bespoke feature windows create a distinctive look. **Right:** An oriel or projecting upper floor window.

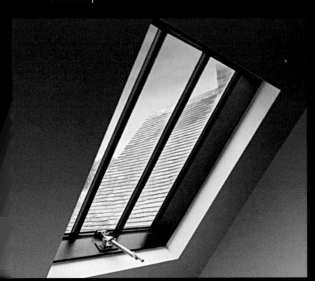

Left: A heritage rooflight, oftrn used in conservation areas. **Right:** Leaded lights in a Tudor building.

DESIGNER NONSENSE

Renovate rather than replace wooden sash windows whenever you can. There are two-part fillers that can be used to rebuild rotten areas, or these areas can be cut out and new wood scarfed into place.

Beware of central pivoting rooflights if you like sleeping in the dark. Blinds fit the window not the frame, and let in light as soon as you open the window. As attic spaces get extremely hot in summer, this is a major design flaw. Fit a top-hinge rooflight instead.

OLD GLASS

Window glass has been around for over 2,000 years but it was not until the early 20th century that the clear, blemish-free, 'float' glass sheets we use today were able to be machine-made and mass-produced, and since then large glass windows have become commonplace.

Before that, glass was mostly handblown so the panes were smaller, with lots of glazing bars in between. Handblown glass is a swirly light-green in colour with small imperfections that make it fascinating to look through. If you're restoring a period or listed property, you can replicate the effect by using handblown glass sheets. They look fabulous in the right property but are, not surprisingly, expensive.

21ST-CENTURY GLASS

Laminated and tempered glass is hard to break and is often used on ground floor areas where security and/or safety is an issue. If you want privacy from a busy road outside, reflective glass coated with metal oxides offers one-way vision without reducing light. Low-emission glass is an energy-efficient option that prevents heat escaping, so good for large expanses of glass. You can also get self-cleaning glass with a chemically bonded surface layer which dissolves dirt under UV light. It is ideal for glass roofs and extensions, although, perhaps, too good to be true.

OBSCURED GLASS

If a neighbour gets a direct view into your house, opaque glass is the answer. There are many more exciting options today than grandma's old-fashioned frosted glass. You can reglaze with sandblasted glass, perhaps with a clear edge or decorative fleur-de-lis-type motif. Alternatively, and less expensive, sticky-back opaque window plastic is an option or glass spray frosting.

STAINED GLASS

Tread carefully before putting in a stained-glass feature window, as low-cost reproductions tend to look exactly that, and commissioning an artist to do a one-off will only appeal to those who share your taste. Stained glass is an investment that you are unlikely to get your return on. However, if you live in a period property with original stained glass doors or windows, look after them well. Such features will always add value to your property.

Opposite: Two luxurious window expanses in a modern property.
Below: The Edwardians knew how to use stained glass to make welcoming hallways.

Window Bars

Basement flats carry with them a heightened security risk as access is easy. So it's a good idea to fit window bars, especially at the front which is often the bedroom. Use well-designed bars with a bit of detailing to fit in with the style of your windows, to avoid your property looking like a prison.

Shutters

Shutters were originally designed to give protection from the elements and to keep intruders out. In Britain they were usually found inside – an excellent reason to think twice before putting them Swiss-chalet style on the outside of your property. They're a feature definitely worth keeping – and worth installing in period properties with good-sized wooden windows in the living areas. Bi-fold shutters give privacy in daytime without sacrificing too much light.

Window Dressing

If you have a really overwhelming desire to get rid of your cash, then go to town on your window dressings. A pair of silk interlined curtains with pelmets, swags, tie-backs, electronic pull cords, rails, fancy finials and the rest can set you back £5,000 plus per window. Whereas you can probably pay less than half that for all the window dressings in a three-bedroom house. Some people spend the money because they think they'll take the curtains with them when they leave. But curtains are relatively non-transferable items. They're always the wrong width or length and end up in a pile in the attic. Nor do elaborate window dressings add to the value of your current property. New owners don't want to pay extra for your taste in curtains. They'd rather put them in the skip. So only go to town on curtains if you will get your money's worth in enjoyment.

THAT LITTLE BIT EXTRA...

French doors, more correctly called French windows, are very effective at bringing the outdoors in. More traditionally, they opened onto the garden from the rear drawing room, but now they're a feature in many kitchen/dining areas.

They work especially well upstairs, opening inwards with a railing-cum-balcony outside. You can also fit sliding and concertina doors that open much wider than French doors would, bringing airy rooftop views inside.

Opposite (above): Open doors bring the tree canopy inside.
Right: Built-in recessed shutters.
Far right: French doors opening onto a tiny balcony.

Adding Space

Kitchen Extensions
Loft Conversions
Conservatories
Basements
Garden Offices & Studios

Moving house is not cheap. A reasonable estimate of the cost is about 10 per cent of the price of the property you're selling. That means if you live in a three-bedroom house worth £300,000 and decide to move into the identical three-bedroom house next door, you'll pay around £30,000 on estate agent's fees, stamp duty, legal costs, removers and the rest. People always underestimate moving costs because they pay them a bit at a time, and don't necessarily add them up.

Trading up to a four-bedroom house, when you include the 'invisible' cost of moving as well as the property price hike, can add a huge whack to your mortgage. How much more sensible, you might think, to hang on to that £30,000 and build an extra room in your current property instead, especially if you like where you are living. Adding square footage will always add value. The only question is whether it adds more value than it costs.

There are three ways to extend: up, out or down. Going up and out – the loft and kitchen/conservatory extensions – are less expensive than going down – the basement. But whichever way you extend, keep the balance of the house. You don't want it to become top- or bottom-heavy, have too many bedrooms for your living space, or wake up and find all your garden inside the conservatory.

When adding space, the finish is everything, so make it the best quality you can afford. You don't always need an architect, but it's a false economy not to on a big project where structure and details count. I'd use a local building company with experience of similar extensions to your style and period of house. You're going to spend serious money on this, so visit previous clients to see how the builders' work stands the test of time.

Before you undergo any building work, check if you need planning permission. Building regulations have recently changed and properties undergoing work are now assessed on their total energy-efficiency. An architect can help.

Kitchen Extensions

A roomy kitchen extension is a huge selling point, but what matters is how well it's been done. Don't tack a box on the back of your house. The kitchen needs to be bold and imaginatively designed so that it creates extra space and uses it to the best effect. You want a chic, light-filled space with subtle but well-defined areas for eating and cooking, not a kitchen that's a corridor to the back garden. It can be traditional or modern, but I'd always put in as much glass as is permitted within building regulations. One spectacular room can sell a house, and for my money a big kitchen full of glazing or, even better, a retractable roof you can open on balmy evenings is a real winner.

SIDE RETURNS

Don't just extend backwards but sideways, too. Those dank, dark passages beside terraced houses – the side return – were probably used by the Victorians on their journey to the outside loo. But today they are wasted space. Extending the kitchen into them makes the layout of a period terrace much more relevant to today's lifestyles. Often the gain in square footage is modest but it makes a huge difference to the room, bringing light through glazing on the roof. You will certainly need to comply with building regulations, who will require you to check weight loads with a structural engineer. The outside wall is generally supporting several floors above and, without the correct support, your house could collapse.

Above: A kitchen extended sidewards with glass roof and units along the outside wall.
Left: The side return is transformed into a light-filled office space.

Nowadays the technology is there to create incredible open ground-floor spaces using portal frames, concealed structural beams and pillars, but it will be costly. If it matters whether you make your money back, check that your postcode can stand it.

THAT LITTLE BIT EXTRA...

It's really worth spending a little extra on really good-quality sliding doors. Personally I can recommend Sunfold doors which run like a hot knife through butter and I would certainly say they are worth every penny.

DESIGNER NONSENSE

It is a fallacy that every kitchen is worth extending. If it eats up your garden, disrupts the balance of your house or looks like a badly-constructed carbuncle, you may knock thousands off the value of your home and make it harder to sell in the current market.

Above: A kitchen extension with folding sliding doors from Sunfold Systems.

Left: This mezzanine floor provides extra space. **Right:** A garden office adds a charming extra room.

Left: A conservatory with an al fresco ambience. **Right:** Cellars are traditionally excellent places to store wine.

Left: Balconies can be added to upper floors. **Right:** Spiral staircases are not always practical but look attractive.

Left: A music room in a garden studio. **Right:** Between inside and out, a perfect space in which to relax.

Left: A light-filled living room extension. **Right:** An upstairs balcony adds space and provides storage underneath.

Left: Extensions can vary in style from the main building. **Right:** A hinged ladder makes loft access easier.

Loft Conversions

Adding square footage is the surest way to add value to a house – just check that you're adding more value than it's going to cost. A loft conversion is a very popular way of creating extra space.

It is generally cheaper per square foot to convert a loft than a kitchen or cellar, as most of the structure is already in place. However, think twice before you indulge your instinct to enlarge it to the max. Changing the profile of the roof by installing dormer windows or a mini-mansard will almost certainly make planning permission less likely. Furthermore, if the installation is badly designed, it can be an eyesore. Alternatively, why not incorporate as much natural light as you can with

rooflights. If you do build a mansard, fitting a pair of glazed doors with railings outside with views over the back garden gives another level of luxury.

One of the most important things to remember for any loft conversion is that it must have sufficient headroom – anything below 7ft at the highest point will feel cramped. Bear in mind, too, that you will lose some of the head height in an attic when converting it to a habitable room, as you will need to strengthen the floor.

STAIRCASES

The way you get into the loft and the detailing of the stairs makes a tremendous difference to the feel and appearance of the conversion. Ideally, the stairs should look as if they are part of the original stairwell, by using similar detailing to that on other floors. Be careful not to use too steep a riser, however, or it will feel as if you are climbing Mt Everest when you go to bed. Straight stairs are less expensive. Open treads, where you see the side of the tread, look very elegant. Use an architect to draw your stairs and then get help from a stairs specialist, such as Southern Staircases.

PLUMBING

I'd strongly advise putting in plumbing and adding an extra bath or shower room on the new floor, especially if the loft is intended as the master bedroom. It keeps the house well-balanced.

Above: A loft converted into a kitchen benefits from good natural light.
Opposite: A bedroom with open-plan en suite makes dramatic use of roof height and beams.

Conservatories

Conservatories can 'bring the outside in' but all too often that translates as boiling in summer, freezing in winter, and leaky. Originally, they were glorified greenhouses for wealthy Victorians in which to store exotic plants from hotter climes, and in a country house, a grand colonial wood and glass conservatory looks wonderful. But a poorly constructed conservatory made from budget materials is more likely to be an under-used eyesore. However, high-tech engineering and glass technology mean that you can create stunning conservatory extensions which, if done to a high standard, will open up the back of your house and add instant glamour and square footage.

There are two ways to go. Traditional hardwood conservatories work well in semis or detached houses with large gardens. You don't have to go bespoke; there are many good off-the-peg designs available. For urban or contemporary houses, a structural

Below: A light-filled glass cube opens the house to the garden.

Above: A traditionally styled conservatory, where tender greenery can thrive, making it part of the garden.

glass cube with fine glazing bars or a frameless glass system will make you feel as if you are having dinner in the garden, but need not be bespoke either. High-ceilinged conservatory extensions are very much in demand and can add enormously to the value of your property. As always, check building regulations and establish whether you need to apply for planning permission, conservation or listed building consent.

TEMPERATURE CONTROL

Conservatories work well on the north or east-face of a property, but south and west-facing conservatories can get intense sun in summer. To maximise year-round comfort, it's vital to control the temperature and light inside. With glass roofs and walls, heat loss is an issue, so use low-emissivity glass that reflects heat out when it's hot, and in when it's cold. It's important to ventilate the roof either electronically with heat sensors, or mechanically with a hand-winder that opens air vents. Motorised blinds, shutters or light-sensitive glass will keep glaring sun away. Blinds from a good-quality supplier, such as Grants Blinds, are well worth the investment if you really want to use the space.

Basements

It's a huge risk putting a basement in a property, and it comes at a high price. Going down is the most expensive and problematic way to extend a home, costing about three times as much per square foot as a loft extension. Whether you make your money back depends on the type of house, the quality of work, the layout, interior design and natural light within the underground space. In pricey areas, where family houses sell for £750,000 or more, a basement is probably a better investment than elsewhere. If your street is full of starter houses or two-up-two-downs, you are unlikely to get your money back on a basement conversion.

Basement extensions are becoming increasingly popular because they can double a house's living space. Many family houses have adequate bedrooms – all those loft conversions – but the ground floor living area is cramped. Building downwards creates a whole extra floor for kitchen or playroom, games room, utility room or guest room, and also liberates space upstairs. But potential problems abound. Foundations may be unsound, and your neighbour's services may be running under your house. Drainage can cause problems, as ground water and waste have to be pumped out upwards from a basement. A lot of properties are built under the water table so with heavy rain and a breach in your tanking – the vital waterproof lining around floor and walls – you could end up with a surprise swimming pool down there.

If you go ahead, keep the ceiling height high – don't settle for less than 8ft – and put in as many sources of natural light as you can via windows, grilles, lightwells, sun tunnels, stairwells and skylights. If you have some extra money, spend it on making a beautiful, open staircase down to the basement – it will transform the space. Finally, expect a long and dirty job, although many basement conversions are carried out through the front garden.

IS YOUR HOUSE SUITABLE?

In theory, you can dig a basement under any house. In practice, some properties are more suitable than others.

- It's easier if you already have a cellar.
- It's easier if you have a suspended timber rather than concrete floor.
- It's harder if your house is constructed on bedrock, which takes longer to cut through.
- If the property is on a flood plain, construction will be much more complex.

ASK THE EXPERTS

It's worth considering using a specialist basement company to do the job for you. They are set up to do exactly this job and, as they do one after another, they are more familiar with problems they might come up against and how to overcome them.

Above opposite: With good detailing a basement can look as though it has always been there (left). Glazed doors pull light down into the basement (right).
Below opposite: A great use for a basement is a utility room, brightened up here by vibrant colours.

Garden Offices & Studios

Most gardens have sheds and they are practical for storing garden equipment. However, today, many of those sheds are being demolished and upmarket garden offices or studios are being put up in their place. This can be a cost-effective way of extending your living area – and it doesn't structurally change your house so, in most cases (see below), you don't need planning permission. It's especially popular in cities such as Brighton and Oxford where, although gardens are small, there is a large population of home workers – one in ten people in London and the south-east now work from home for part of the week – and many don't have the space in the house to carve out a dedicated office area. It's practical and useful to have an extra room or two in your garden, and it definitely adds saleability and value to a property. The key is to make the space flexible and dual-purpose, and not to stint on your services. Electricity, heating and broadband are a must.

Traditional or modern, most garden studios are made of wood and glass and are well insulated and energy-efficient. You can design and build yourself, buy off-the-peg or get a bespoke version from a specialist contractor, who'll look after everything from foundations to finish. Some come with decks and verandahs which are delightfully quaint.

PLANNING IMPLICATIONS

You don't normally need planning permission for a garden studio unless you're living in a conservation area or listed building. Although you need to comply with the following:

- It must be at least 5m from your house and 1m from the boundary.
- A building cannot be more than 4m high if you have a ridge, or 3m in any other case.
- If you intend to use it as a permanent dwelling with sleeping quarters, full building regulations apply and you need to get planning permission.

Below: A peaceful, multi-functional garden room high up in the trees.

Above and below: Garden studios make great use of the space at the bottom of town gardens.

Flooring

Carpets
Wooden Flooring
Natural Stone Floors
Ceramic Tiles
Mosaic Floors
Linoleum and Vinyl
Rubber
Glass

The effect of flooring on the design of a room cannot be underestimated. Good-quality hard floors, or well-fitted carpet with good underlay, can make a tremendous difference to the finish – and therefore the value – of a property. Yet flooring is often left until the final stages of a project and treated as a bit of an afterthought. Plan ahead. It can take six to eight weeks to arrive and eat up a significant lump of the money. I'd expect the flooring in a three- or four-bedroom property to cost anywhere up to £10,000 – not a sum to be overlooked.

Ideally, flooring is designed so that one surface flows seamlessly into another, especially around hallways, stairs and other transitional areas. It's always a good idea to think about the surfaces you want to use early in the design stage, to minimise problems later. For example, if you're laying underfloor heating, there are certain floorings, including solid wood, that are best avoided. Also often forgotten is a sunken recess for a doormat inside front and back doors. Ideally, a mat should be big enough for at least two steps inside the house.

The flooring in access areas needs to be sturdy and practical. Many years ago, rushes were used to protect wood floors and keep dirt down. Many modern wood floors are easily scratched and dented, so wear badly in areas of heavy foot traffic. The Victorians cleverly used tessellated tile floors in hallways, which are hardwearing and don't show dirt. However, two muddy steps and a contemporary limestone floor is just a mess.

It's a myth that using the same floor covering throughout a property makes it feel bigger. In fact, the opposite is often true. It's much more interesting to use different but complementary floor coverings to lead the eye through different rooms and floors and give an illusion of space.

Carpets

Carpets have had bad press over recent years, which is a shame for the industry but also very unjust because, let's be honest, they are incredibly nice to live with. Some people claim that wooden floors make a house more saleable, but they can also feel cool and soulless. I think all bedrooms should have fitted carpets and given half the chance I would put carpet in bathrooms too.

Carpet has many benefits. It makes a space look luxurious and cosy. It's warm and comfortable to walk and sit on, and eliminates the foot-traffic clatter which can drive you mad with wooden floors. Fitted carpets keep rooms warmer, too, so you use less energy heating the house. Admittedly, any badly stained carpet looks awful – I'd replace before selling a property.

There are some stunningly good carpets around. A good carpet supplier will have a vast and varied selection. The look you get depends on how the carpet is made. Woven carpets like Wilton and Axminster – which are methods of construction, not just manufacturers – are longer-lasting, denser and more luxurious underfoot. Tufted carpet, where yarn is looped through a pre-woven backing into tufts, is quicker and cheaper to make and comes in velvet, twisted or looped pile finishes. A 100 per cent wool is lovely to touch though marginally less hardwearing than wool mixes. Other natural fibres, such as sisal, coir, seagrass and jute, look good in the right place but can feel harsh underfoot.

If you can't get your head around fitted carpets, a good compromise is to have wood floors with the comfort of a non-fitted

Below: This traditionally styled carpet adds colour and comfort to a country house bedroom.

carpet or rug on top. Don't forget that most floorboards in period properties were never meant to be on view. You can get free-standing carpets with amazing edging in contrasting colours or materials like leather. Or, for real living room glamour, lay wooden floors with a sunken carpeted area in the middle, where everyone can chill out in luxury and comfort.

PATTERNED CARPETS

Although for a long time now they have been considered rather unfashionable, patterned carpets are making a comeback. After all, they are tremendously practical and don't show the dirt, which is why they tend to be laid in pubs and hotels. Patterned carpet is one of the best ways to get texture into a room. As with clothing, big patterns in contrasting colours draw attention; small patterns give a subtle background. Look at the room as a whole: if all your furniture has soft, curvy edges, a straight-lined geometric-patterned carpet will look out of place. Patterned Persian rugs, meanwhile, are timelessly beautiful, especially on wooden or stone floors.

RUNNERS

If you want to make a feature of a dull, straight stairway, runners are the answer. They come in fabulous colours and patterns, and produce a very different effect depending on the rods you choose (wood, stainless steel, brass, bronze, etc) and how you stain or paint the stair edgings. Stair rods also make a narrow staircase look wider.

Above: The bright stripes of this carpet runner complement the oak staircase.
Right: Hardwearing sisal carpeting, stripped skirting boards and doors, unify the look.

Left: Steel rods keep this carpet runner in place. **Right:** An alternative bath mat made from bamboo.

Left: Black and white tiles make a strong statement. **Right:** Marble flooring and stairs provide a grand entrance.

Left: A contemporary twist on a classic design. **Right:** Carpet runner on a parquet floor mixes old and new.

Left: Dark wooden floorboards for a traditional-style bedroom. Right: Good mosaics are works of art.

Left: Rubber flooring is hardwearing and practical. Right: An Axminster carpet adds to the cosy atmosphere here.

Wooden Flooring

Wood flooring has been incredibly popular for the past ten years and many buyers currently prefer it to carpet. But although it may help with a property's saleability it may not add much value, so think carefully before splashing out on the most expensive solid wood floors. It is also incredibly noisy and you may need to carry out alternative sound-proofing in an upstairs flat. Check your lease before you get rid of carpets – many don't allow hardwood floors to be laid.

If you're in a period property and want a wooden floor, take up the carpets and have a look at the floorboards underneath. In most Victorian and Edwardian houses, floorboards were covered and they may not be of very high quality but, if they are, you can sand, fill and stain them. Bear in mind which way floorboards are laid as they pull the eye with them.

Otherwise, there are various options:

- **Solid wood flooring** consists of solid planks of wood, often with a tongue-and-groove fit, sometimes nailed on top of a wooden sub-floor. Reclaimed or new, it's expensive but always looks luxurious and can be repeat-sanded so should last for generations. It may warp in humid or hot conditions.
- **Engineered wood flooring** consists of three or more core layers of wood/ply, with a real wood veneer stuck on top. The plywood layers make it more resilient to moisture and heat, so it is more suitable for laying on concrete sub-bases or with underfloor heating.
- **Solid bamboo flooring** is an eco-friendly option as it is fast-growing, cheaper than wood, but with the moisture and heat resilience of engineered wood flooring.
- **Laminate flooring** is not wood at all, but an image of wood laid over a fibreboard base sealed with acrylic. Although a great deal cheaper than other floorings, it looks dull and lifeless. It is best only for the budget end of the market.

Solid and engineered wood floors come prefinished with polyurethane seals and lacquers, or unfinished so you can treat it with oil or wax-based finishes to give a natural look.

Above: Floorboards in the hallway of the 18th-century Staircase Hall created by John Chute at the The Vyne, Hampshire. **Opposite:** An historic room in Chatsworth House, Derbyshire, with parquet flooring.

PARQUET AND MARQUETRY

Parquet flooring – where wooden blocks are laid in patterns to create a herringbone or basketweave effect – was used in grand Jacobean houses but became highly popular with the Victorians. If you're lucky enough to have a parquet floor, treat it with respect. They can be really beautiful and will enhance the value of your home. You can buy reclaimed parquet for about the same price as solid wood flooring, but be aware it needs skill to lay it. At the top end of the market, consider installing a specialist parquet floor. In large hallways or reception rooms, Versailles panels – 1m square parquet blocks with a border around – look fabulous.

Marquetry is a old skill which inlays different veneers into wood to create a picture or decorative effect. New laser techniques mean that it's cheaper than ever before. Geometric shapes, compasses or stars are often used as centrepieces, and marquetry borders look dramatic around the outer edges of a room.

Natural Stone Floors

By the 17th century, stone-flagging, marble, brick and quarry tiles began to be widely used. Today, we still use these natural materials because they are timeless, look good in contemporary or classic interiors, are incredibly durable. They add character and interest to a home and – unlike most carpets – improve with age. Now that stone can be cut to thicknesses of 15mm, it can even be laid on upper floors, though you should check with a structural engineer first before doing this.

Natural stone – marble, limestone, sandstone, slate – can be expensive, but it can be a rock solid investment for your property. As long as you aren't too much of a fashion victim with a stone floor, it will look great for a long time to come. It is ideal for the upper end of the market.

Stone for floors usually comes in two finishes: riven – a slightly rough surface that looks good in rustic kitchens; and honed, which has a smooth matt finish. Polished stone is slippery and scratches badly, so think carefully before using it for flooring, especially in high-traffic areas.

There has been a flurry of fashion around pale limestone in recent years. People buy it because they love its light, reflective qualities but it is extremely porous and you have to be aware of its limitations. Leave a little red wine on even a sealed limestone floor for a few hours and no amount of vigorous scrubbing will lift the stain. If you choose to lay limestone, therefore, you have to accept

Above left: Brick flooring in a Spanish-style kitchen with an antique wooden unit.
Left: Modern stone flooring has been laid throughout the downstairs of this property.

it is soon going to look weathered and worn – that's the joy of it. All stone surfaces are porous to some extent, so slather on two or three coats of invisible sealant before you use them, and reseal every year.

THAT LITTLE BIT EXTRA...

The bigger the pieces of slate or stone you use, the more expensive and luxurious it looks. That goes for wood width, too. If you have space, large slabs of natural materials are the ultimate luxury.

Below: Old stone flagstones have been retained in this period property.

DESIGNER REMINDERS

Stone can be cold to the touch but it also stores heat extremely well so underfloor heating is ideal.

Stuff breaks on stone when you drop it, so it's not the most practical surface for young children.

Stone is a natural resource created over millions of years, so we should use it responsibly – after all, there is a only a finite amount of it.

Ceramic Tiles

Originally just flattened bricks of sun-dried clay, tiles have been used on floors and roofs for thousands of years. When glazed and fired at high temperatures they become water-resistant and very hard to break. Unglazed quarry tiles and thin, brick-shaped paviours were laid in kitchen areas in Britain from the 17th century, and in Victorian times glazed geometric tiles became incredibly popular for hallways and kitchens. Nowadays, the range of styles is enormous, allowing you to create any style, from Edwardian parlour to Moroccan palace, within a reasonable budget.

Above: A Victorian hallway featuring an original encaustic tile floor. These attractive unglazed tiles can also often be seen in exterior pathways. **Below:** Quarry tiles tend to suit more traditional rooms.

Mosaic floors

Mosaics use tiny pieces of glass, stone or pebbles to make decorative pictures or patterns. Some of the most stunning and dramatic interiors over the ages have used floor mosaics, but great mosaics are an art form. You can now get much simpler section stick-on mosaics, but these need to be perfectly laid so as not to look terrible. If you want a great mosaic floor, your only option is to commission one. However, remember, with such a specific look, it may not add much to the value of your property.

LAYING TILES

The way you lay tiles in a room has a dramatic impact. There are many traditional tile patterns – herringbone, basketweave, broken joint, checkerboard, railroad – which use two or more different sizes, shapes or colours of tile to produce an interesting multi-dimensional effect. Whether you lay tiles straight or diagonal within the space depends on your room. Laying straight will look dreadfully messy unless your walls are totally square. So in old houses it is usually better to lay diagonally and use smaller tiles, which are more forgiving of irregularities. A border gives a room a finished look but can bring the walls in visually. Keep borders simple, especially in a relatively small room where there are lots of different shapes. Although wide tiles are currently fashionable, they don't work well in narrow hallways. You need a repeat of four or more tiles across a hall to get real impact. If you're laying yourself, use tiles with self-spacing lugs to give an even grout line. Porous tiled floors such as slate, marble and unglazed terracotta should be sealed before laying. Many ceramic tile floors are also sealed with an acrylic top coat to protect them and lengthen their life.

Above: White ceramic floor tiles may seem impractical but when dirty at least they are easy to clean.

GROUTING

Floor tiles are most often removed not because they're worn or broken but because the grouting looks filthy. The colour of grout is crucial: it comes in a range of shades from terracotta to ivory via charcoal and stone, to suit most floorings. Sometimes a contrasting grout is a bold feature: slate with a white grout looks entirely different from grey. Tiles can be laid bumper to bumper with almost no grout lines and can look elegant, but you need a very good surface to lay on. Thicker grout lines are more forgiving and allow for floor movement and flexibility. Sealing the whole floor once it is laid, especially the grout lines, will keep grout waterproof and dirt-free for longer.

Linoleum and Vinyl

Every time I think sensibly about a floor covering, I end up with lino. It is the most practical flooring, full stop. In a kitchen or bathroom, you just can't fault it. It's waterproof, long-lasting, protective, low-maintenance, easy to lay, and covers up any irregularities on the surface below. Children and crockery bounce on it. It comes in many colours and patterns, and is a doddle to clean. It's silly that it gets such a bad press, but that's partly because lino designs are often a bit uninspired. It has a long history. In the 17th and 18th centuries, floors were covered with canvas cloth which was painted and varnished in layers to protect the wood below. This was the forerunner of lino, an entirely natural product made from solidified linseed oil, limestone, pine rosin and pigments on a jute backing. Invented in 1863, it was hugely popular as a practical low-cost floor covering for 100 years, then surpassed by vinyl. But as a green, biodegradable product that decomposes naturally and is desperately practical, I predict it will soon be making a comeback.

Cushioned polyvinyl flooring arrived big time in the 1960s and still remains popular because it is generally cheap, hardwearing and waterproof – so makes good sense in bathrooms and kitchens. However, it is not at all environmentally friendly, being made of PVC resin mixed with plasticisers and other additives. Today, upmarket vinyl flooring comes in an extraordinary range of effects, from glitter to stone and wood, mosaic and marble. Although, in most properties, I can't help thinking it would be more cost-effective to spend the money on natural flooring, which always appeals to a broad range of buyers, despite it being a little less practical.

Rubber

Rubber is another hardwearing floor covering which is becoming increasingly popular because it looks modern and funky, is bouncy underfoot, and environmentally friendly in its manufacture and disposal. It comes in studded and plain tiles and sheets, or in liquid form, which can be poured, in a variety of vibrant colours – though not white, which apparently looks rather like grubby chewing gum.

Glass

Hugely expensive – from about £250 per square metre, plus structural and fitting costs – glass flooring is probably best used in small areas to bring light to dingy hallways or rooms below. It can be acid-etched and sandblasted in finishes such as dots and stripes to make it opaque and non-slip, and tinted in blues, greens, yellows and reds as well as clear. It looks stunning, but comes at a cost and is very expensive to remove, so don't lay it unless it is absolutely right for your market.

DESIGNER NONSENSE

Don't be fooled when someone tries to tell you that your chosen floor covering will hide imperfections in the sub-floor. The opposite is true. The finish of your floor will only ever be as good as the sub-floor.

Above left: Black and white economical vinyl flooring. Above right: Stone-coloured vinyl floor tiles in this hallway.
Below left: Linoleum is making a comeback in modern interiors. Below right: Hard-wearing rubber flooring.

Colour & Paint

It's been fashionable for several years to paint homes in natural tones such as stone, beige, off-white and grey. In the early 1990s, trendy walls were painted bold, sun-soaked shades inspired by the Mediterranean and Far East. Whereas the 1980s housed a load of paint effects and fleurs-de-lis. Fashions in colour are cyclical, which means if we live long enough we will undoubtedly see the avocado bathroom suite making a comeback. No doubt renamed 'sage lavatory'.

Wallpaper is making a slow comeback into fashion, mainly because it tends to be a more skillful job to hang well than to paint and so, generally, walls are still painted. And there are more fashion paint ranges than ever before. Colour reference libraries such as NCS and RAL have 4,000 to 6,000 colours each; the human eye can hardly tell the difference between some of them. Today, Dulux offers 1,200 colours including the chance to mix your own in store. With so many to choose from, it is increasingly difficult to pick a way through and find the absolute winning shades for your design.

Natural shades can look rich and complex, but they can also look bland and uninspiring. In terms of selling a property, bland is probably safer than a shocking colour, but you can still be bold. Paint is an inexpensive and easy way to transform a room. The key is to educate yourself first about colour. Some people have a natural eye for colour, but if you're not born with it you can train your eye to be more inspired and daring. Look at books and magazines to get ideas of which colours work together. Try to picture the whole room in your head. Bear in mind that colours that look fantastic on clothes or a car, may not translate so well to walls. With a load of research under your belt you should have the confidence to be that little bit bolder in order to create a more sophisticated end design.

Choosing Colours

Personally, I've always had a bit of a problem with the concept of 'taste' as it is entirely subjective. Whether yours is good or bad is a matter of opinion. However, some colour design will appeal to a broad spectrum of people's 'personal taste', and if you are selling a property it makes sense to tread this design path. There is a science to a great deal of design, though, and if your colour flair is not so inspired, resorting to the science of colour is a very wise thing to do.

The colour of something is made up of its hue (what makes it red and not green), luminance (brightness or darkness) and saturation (how intense or strong it is). Each of the three elements affects how colours relate to one another. Dark, high-saturation colours, such as orange-red, 'advance' in a

Below: A cosy atmosphere in this country cottage is created by an absence of white paint.

room and are considered lively and exciting. They make specifically painted areas within large spaces feel intimate, and small spaces feel cosy and den-like. But they also make the space appear smaller.

Low-saturation colours, such as violet-blue, 'recede' in a room and are considered soft, serene and quiet. In bright tints, they make good backgrounds for living areas, allowing pictures or other focal points to take centre stage. They also make a room appear bigger.

Receding colours 'raise' the ceiling height, and the effect is increased if a receding colour is also used on the floor, with advancing colour on the walls.

Dark, highly saturated, advancing colours 'lower' the ceiling height, and the effect is increased if an advancing colour is also used on the floor, with receding colour on the walls.

To make a room look longer, paint the far wall in a receding colour. Paint a distant wall an advancing colour and it will seem closer.

Minimalism in its purest form played around with the concepts of colour, taking full advantage of the science behind it.

PAINT SAMPLES

Paint sample pots are a godsend for anyone trying to pick a colour. They may seem pricey but work out less expensive than buying a whole tin of paint and hating it once it is on the wall. When designing decoration, it's important to realise that picking a colour from a printed swatch is rather like going to a hairdresser asking for a Jennifer Aniston cut, then being disappointed when you don't look like her afterwards. Your hair might, but the whole package does not. It's the same with paint colours. They never look the same on the wall as they do on the chart because colour is massively affected by

Above: Bright yellow and purple provide a bold statement.

the other colours that are beside it, as well as by changing light in a room.

To find a colour scheme that works, I suggest using A1 and A4 sheets of hardboard or cardboard. Paint all the colours you're thinking of using on walls, ceiling and woodwork on the A4 sheets. Stand them in the room for a few days, moving them around so you see them next to each other in all kinds of daylight and electric light, and alongside the other fittings, flooring and furniture. Whittle down the choices to a few and paint these colours onto the larger A1 board. Mull the colours over for as long as you can. It's not foolproof, but a more considered paint choice is likely to give you a better end result.

Left: Lime green with a sheen for a bathroom. Right: Poppy red is a warm 'advancing' colour.

Left: Delicate midnight butterfly wallpaper. Right: Walls and units painted in similar tones for a complete look.

Left: A muted shade of pink sets off the furnishings. Right: Dark brown tones compliment a dark wood kitchen.

Left: Bright green is a backdrop for an ornate headboard. Right: Detail from a wallpaper with a traditional design.

Left: Don't be afraid to be bold with paint. Right: Here, woodwork has been painted with a matt finish.

White and Off-White

Although many people may not believe it, white is actually one of the hardest colours to get right. You may think it's a simple choice between white and off-white. But pure white is very bold and cold, and highly-reflective white gloss can be tiring on the eye. That's why every paint company has a range of at least 20 or so off-white tints and shades with pink, yellow, blue, green, brown and black in them. These complex whites absorb and reflect light and pick up hues from neighbouring colours in a more responsive way.

When you're choosing an off-white, think of the 'warmth' factor you want in the room: earth-toned whites have a warm vibe while blue or grey tones give a cool sharpness. If you're using colour with a buffer white next to it, don't feel you have to use brilliant white. But be aware the white you chose has to complement all the other paint colours in the room in terms of hue, brightness and saturation. Sharp, cold whites don't tend to work terribly well with warm colours, and vice versa. However, with off-whites I think you can be more daring than the shade you naturally verge towards. As a general rule, be daring, as bolder looks better.

Paint Finishes

The way light reflects from a coloured surface affects the way we see it. With interior paints there are various finishes which bring different qualities to a room.

Gloss is highly reflective, and the shinier the finish, the easier it is to wipe down. Boldly coloured gloss looks fantastic on walls, but it gives a very strong look and is unforgiving to a poorer wall finish – so if in doubt, don't use it. Until about ten years

ago, gloss paint tended to be used on woodwork but nowadays a lower sheen finish is more fashionable.

Satin/eggshell gives a hard but low-sheen finish rather similar to the shell of an egg, hence the name. It's good for interior woodwork and is more durable and hardwearing than a matt surface. It is less reflective than gloss and can be lightly scrubbed, so is good for areas of wear such as doors and skirting boards.

Matt is a more forgiving surface to the eye than gloss because the light will not catch imperfections. It's a very traditional look – old houses were always painted with distemper or limewash before the arrival of emulsion paint. Light is absorbed by a matt finish so it gives a soft, diffuse look which is very restful on the eye. However, it is not hardwearing and tends to need touching up regularly.

Textured paints are often used to cover or bind together a poor wall finish. If you want a smooth wall finish, you have two choices: hack off the plaster and start again, or try skimming over the texture. Although, beware, if the plaster beneath is at the end of its life, you are unlikely to get a perfect finish without hacking it off.

Above: Black gloss walls provide a strong background in this eclectic dining room. **Opposite:** Two examples of different shades of white – a hint of grey (above) and a creamy shade of white (below).

Above: Various textures of the same colour on the woodwork and flooring for a unified look.

Designer Ranges

If you want guidance through the minefield of colour, you could do worse than to pick paint from a designer brand you like. Designer ranges offer an edited selection of colours that tend to work well together, thus saving you time if not money. However, be careful about picking and mixing from different ranges – a subtle, chalky Farrow & Ball colour will look very odd next to the sharp, bright tones in the Designers Guild range.

On the other hand, you may not want to spend an arm and a leg on paint, in which case look at the extensive ranges of own-brand and high-street manufacturers. Generally, light, neutral colours are excellent in the big brand ranges. Paint is inexpensive when there is less pigment, which makes most difference when you are trying to achieve deep colours such as dark reds or greens. Cheaper paints with added fillers have the bonus of being more durable and easier to clean, and may need fewer coats than thinner, more expensive paints. However, be aware that you won't tend to get the same depth of colour or sophisticated chalky finish.

Woodwork

Personally, I would always resist painting white gloss on woodwork. In fact, I would resist white woodwork full stop. Although many believe that it's the only colour for the job, in fact there is no great historical precedent for it. Blue-greens, olives, chocolates, black and dark off-whites all look punchier than white. In really rich-looking rooms, the woodwork – wainscotting, skirting, doors, dado and picture rails – are often painted in different

DESIGNER REMINDERS

If you have a passion for exciting colours, go for it. But think it through in terms of the whole room. Just randomly painting your walls orange may not create the desired effect, leaving you disappointed.

It takes seven to 12 years for a colour to work its way through the interiors trend cycle (compared to just two years in fashion). We could soon find ourselves at the end of neutrals.

On the B&Q website (diy.com), there is an interactive room planner where you can upload a picture of your room and try out various paints and wallcoverings.

Above: On a stairway you can afford to use vibrant colours; broken shades of acidic greeney-yellow have been used for dramatic emphasis. **Below**: In stark contrast, this woodwork is a muted shade of matt greeney-blue.

Left: Distressed paint effects provide a unique finish. **Right:** Colourwashed walls and ceiling in a traditional hallway. **Below left:** Black woodwork contrasts with light walls. **Below right:** Natural shades work well here.

but complementary colours to the walls, ceiling and cornicing, giving an almost baroque look. Or go for strong coloured woodwork with light walls – it can look sensational. However, there is a caveat. When you are bold with colour it's easier to make mistakes, so put a lot of thought into it before you start.

Paint Effects

Very large wall spaces can look dull painted a single colour. Decorative paint effects solve the problem by bringing depth and texture to a wall – and also have the benefit of disguising less than perfect surfaces. Most paint effect techniques are simple in theory but complex to master, and involve 'colour building' by washing thin layers of paint or glaze over a background colour. Using a rag, chamois leather, sponge or spatter brush will give different effects. If you are going to 'have a go' yourself, I would recommend experimenting on pieces of hardboard before you start, as poorly executed paint effects are not great to look at. Marbling, graining and faux finishes are harder to achieve, and so it's best to get a professional in. But be warned, few people are truly skilled in this age-old art. Most decorators are more likely to dip a broom in the paint and sweep the walls rather than execute lovingly handcrafted trompe l'oeil scenes or a faux Siena marble wall. But the 'old school' traditionally trained decorator can make it look stunning.

What's in Paint?

The amount of volatile organic compounds (VOCs) in paints is currently under review. VOCs, primarily solvents or oils, are added

to give a better finish. They allow paint to dry more slowly so uneven brush strokes and other irregularities are levelled out – almost like a cake mixture levels out in a tin. However, VOCs can cause respiratory problems and neurological damage in high doses. They also evaporate into the atmosphere causing an increase in greenhouse gases. Basically, the more unpleasant a paint smells, the more VOCs it contains, and the worse it will be for your health.

To stop us from killing ourselves and damaging the environment, new EU legislation comes into force in 2010 to limit the amount of VOCs allowed in paint. As a result, many new water-based paints are coming on to the market. Contrary to what many people think, a well-applied water-based paint is just as hardwearing and long-lasting as an oil-based paint and has the advantage of not yellowing with age. Some eco-paint manufacturers produce paint that is completely free of VOCs, though these can be tricky to actually use. B&Q's entire range of own-brand paints already contain minimal VOCs below the new EU level.

Wallpaper

Although for the past 20 years printed wallpaper has been relatively unfashionable, it has been making a comeback. People are now hanging boldly designed wallpapers, reminiscent of the ones we were putting up in the 1970s and stripping off in the 1980s. Wallpaper can add colour, pattern and texture in a dramatic and adventurous way, making a property stand out from the crowd. However, there are some shockers out there that should be steered clear of. I would steer clear of most of the wallpaper available from high-street chains. It is washable and forgiving of imperfect wall surfaces, but it is a poor

Above: Morris wallpaper is still available – this design is called Willow Bough.

imitation of traditional wallpapers such as Lincrusta, and does not create the grand and luscious look it aspires to. Geometric shapes bring energy, while small patterns work well in smaller areas. Natural fibres like cork, cloth, silk and string give background texture. However, the four walls of a room are a very large area upon which to impose a dominant metallic floral finish, so tread lightly. Although taste is a personal thing, you don't want to make buyers wince.

HANGING WALLPAPER

Although everyone thinks they can paint a wall, it is an absolute certainty that the majority of people cannot hang wallpaper well. The first time I papered a room it had as many bubbles as an Aero bar, and there was nothing to do except pull it off and start again. There is a skill to wallpapering, and if you have not acquired it my advice is to get someone else to do it with or for you. Badly hung wallpaper looks absolutely shocking. However, manufacturers are developing techniques to make wallpaper easier to hang. Today, many wallpapers are designed to enable you to paste the wall not the paper, although these are only available in limited ranges.

A BRIEF HISTORY

Decorating walls with paper was a Chinese custom which reached Europe in 1481, when the King of France commissioned a wallpaper of angels against a blue background for one of his palaces. In 16th- and 17th-century Britain, wallhangings were made from shredded cloth and patterned with stencilled flowers, animals and heraldry.

In the 18th century, expensive Chinese wallpaper with elaborate scenes of birds

Above: Hand-made, early 19th-century Chinese wallpaper in the Chinese room at Burton Constable Hall, an Elizabethan mansion in Yorkshire. The background colour was originally face-powder pink but has faded over time.

and flowers became sought after for the drawing rooms and bedrooms of the wealthy and fashionable, and can still be seen in many country houses around the country today.

In 1864, William Morris produced his first handblocked wallpaper, while mechanisation meant that cheaper geometric-patterned papers were soon available to a wider market. In the 19th century, printed rolls of wallpaper were first manufactured. The Victorians developed Lincrusta and Anaglypta – paintable imitation plasterwork and embossed wood-effect wallpapers, which are still often used, mainly below the dado rail in period houses.

THAT LITTLE BIT EXTRA...

Handpainted or embossed wallpaper is fabulous, but you will pay through the nose for it…

Vistas

The most enticing properties tend to be those with space – or, if not actual space, then the illusion of it. The tremendously high price of square footage in this country means that we squash in add-on 'rooms' – a computer desk on a landing, a 1.5m en suite pinched from the now-tiny second bedroom – which are undeniably useful but sometimes make a home feel cramped. If we don't use every available inch of space, we think it's a waste. But in fact 'wasted' space is rarely wasted. To be able to have a roomy hallway, corridor or stairwell is a sign of real luxury. And if you haven't got them, clever design can help you create a sense of spaciousness that makes your property stand out from the crowd.

Try an experiment. Walk through your front door and examine how far you can see. If you can catch a glimpse of the garden at the back, the sky through a rooflight in the stairwell, or an interesting-looking room to the side or at the top of the stairs, then you have great sight lines which give a sense of openness, an intriguer as to what is beyond. But if you are confronted by high corridors or walls and blank, featureless doors, you're boxed in and the space immediately seems smaller than it really is.

Creating sight lines or views within a property is crucial, and can transform it from dull functionality to breezy spaciousness. Quite simply, the further you can see, the bigger it feels. One good trick to achieve it is to design the transitional areas as interlinking rooms in themselves, with their own entity. If you have an alcove in a passageway, make a feature of it by putting a collection – pictures of family or old maps of the world – to make people stop and say, 'look at that!'. Light corridors in a fantastic way, with glorious chandeliers or creative lighting set into the stairs. Use mirrors to bounce a line of sight off into the distance, so at first glance you can believe a hallway goes on for ever.

And if all else fails, I'd always think about restructuring the ground floor layout. It's definitely worth altering the position of doors or creating sliding openings to give good sight lines, especially in a property's entrance area.

Entry Points

People see porches and hallways as wasted space. But walking straight into a room from the street has its disadvantages, for example when you're sitting on the sofa in your underwear and someone you live with opens the door to the postman. The transition space from outside to inside is a place to get the mud off your feet and dispense with coats and outside gear, as well as a barrier between you and the delivery man. It's also the first view of the rest of your home.

In terms of décor, there are sight lines leading from the entry point through every open door. So if people catch a glimpse of a yellow room then a pink and blue room, the effect will look rather like a paint chart. The colours of the rooms and the linking space between should co-ordinate. That doesn't mean sticking to white or a palette of bland neutrals, but pulling together different but complementary wall colours, floorings, patterns and textures to suggest each room you see is part of a co-ordinated whole.

STAIRCASES

You can really muck up a transitional area with a badly designed staircase. People often place them without much thought to how they will be used. But staircases control the traffic flow and sight lines in a property, and can be beautifully constructed items of sculpture in their own right. It's disappointing if they just get you from one place to another, so make them visually interesting. Detailing is crucial. With period staircases, cut strings – where you can see the end of the tread from the open side of the staircase – look hugely stylish. Try painting the balusters something other than white.

A new contemporary staircase can completely change the look of a house. It will be expensive but, if you have money to spend on an item, this should be it. In terms of longevity, think twice before being a victim to fashion – any look that is very 'in' now will probably soon be very 'out'. And don't forget the views to the top of the staircase. If you can, create some interest like a landing, window, rooflight or open door to entice the eye upstairs.

MOVING WALLS

Traditional room dividers are incredibly useful. But the most efficient way of opening up rooms is with moving walls, which transform spaces and sight lines by bringing light and interest into gloomy corridors and halls. They are essentially

DESIGNER NONSENSE

People think spiral staircases are space savers, but they take up more room than most conventional staircases and are annoyingly difficult to get anything (furniture, coffee cups, yourself) up and down. However, they look quaint. I'd use a metal spiral staircase in a garden setting, leading down outside from an upstairs room. It can double as a fire escape, too.

Below: A collection of hats on display high up gives this hall sight lines and character.

sliding sections fitted into partition walls – choose ones that roll back within the wall cavity and maximise space by disappearing altogether. They come in wood, clear, sandblasted or mirrored glass and in a range of contemporary frames. Moving walls may not be right for many period homes as they are much easier to build in a property built from scratch, but they can transform the often-cramped hallways and corridors of modern apartments and houses. Partly open, they create interest as you look through to the scene beyond. And thrown wide, they bring corridor space into the room to make the area bigger. Just don't scrimp on the mechanism – a rough-running sliding door is insufferable.

Above: A view is broken up with simple display units. **Left:** A classic hall with a view.

Left: Wood burning stoves are ideal focal points. **Right:** Arches and columns provide classic detailing.

Left: An elaborate highly detailed mirror. **Right:** Luxurious, stainless steel bench radiator with a wenge wood seat.

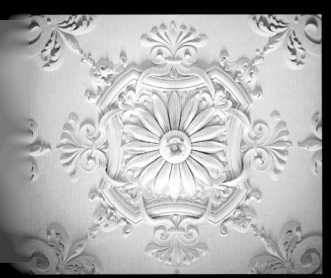

Left: Carved marble panel in the Dolma Bahche Palace, Istanbul. Right: Original fittings add personality.

Left: Antique metal decorative door handles. Right: Detailed cornicing is a great benefit.

Above: Plasterwork arch and broken pedimented doorway at Peckover House. A carved eagle surmounts the pediment.

Small Details

You can't fit much furniture in transitional areas, so the eye is naturally drawn to other small areas of detailing. In Georgian and Victorian homes, hallways and corridors were packed with elaborate detail, from cornicing, columns, alcoves and arches to dado rails and ceiling roses. Detailing makes a property individual but it can also have a useful 'Alice in Wonderland' effect: the bigger you make the small details, the bigger a room appears.

CORNICING

If you have original decorative plasterwork in a property, treat it with respect. People used to rip out cornicing because it looked heavy and old-fashioned, but below the layers of paint many cornices are rather delicate and beautiful decorations. If they're cracked or broken, they can be copied and repaired. Otherwise, careful cleaning will restore them to crisp relief and highlight their detail. If you're thinking of putting new cornicing in, make sure it is the appropriate period for the house. Reproduction architectural detailing has to be believable, so sticking up a cheap polystyrene cornice or ceiling rose will never look right.

SKIRTING

At the bottom of interior walls, most properties have skirting boards. Wood and marble skirting became commonplace in the 18th century, to give a protective finish to newly fashionable plastered walls. Today, you can change the look of a room by the height, width and detailing of the skirting you choose. Shallow chamfered skirting looks sleek, while tall, ornate S-shaped ogee and torus mouldings give greater visual depth. You can lay the same type of wood skirting as wood floor – most manufacturers sell both, but it can be a bit heavy. In minimalist interiors, skirting boards are dispensed with completely, and a lovely straight line of plaster sits a little above the floor. It's a fantastic effect which makes the walls appear to float.

DADO & PICTURE RAILS

The dado rail or chair rail was a practical yet attractive way to protect walls from chair backs scraping against them. Perhaps because nowadays we have more robust paint finishes, you rarely see dado rails in modern houses. By the 17th century, walls were divided horizontally into sections along classical proportions, and the dado separated the lower or lying panel, often wainscotted with wooden panelling, from the large, plain panel above. A picture or frieze rail usually lay above that. These sections can break up the wall space in a pleasing way, but are also extremely practical décor-wise. If you want to use a heavy patterned wallpaper or strong paint colour, apply it below the dado rail so as to prevent it from dominating. Picture rails are underused today and their original use of

Below: Restored cornicing and double panelled doors in a period property with a contemporary feel.

hanging artwork from them was very sensible as it means that you can move it around without peppering your wall with holes.

Focal Points

Every well-designed room should have at least one focal point. It attracts attention to a chosen area and, just as useful, diverts it from others. Often a focal point is fixed, like a fireplace, but it can be as simple as an artwork or gorgeous light-fitting. For period properties, salvage yards are a good place to find unusual focal points that will add value to your home.

FIREPLACES
If you're replacing a fireplace, beware of marketing. The budget reproduction fireplace called 'Victoriana' may bear no relation to anything seen in a Victorian house (see page 166 for a genuine Victorian fireplace). Original period fireplaces tend to be pricey, and good reproductions only marginally less so. Go with an original if you can afford it, then an incredibly good imitation of an original, or go with contemporary. Now that fireplaces are not the primary source of heat, contemporary fireplaces can hang from ceilings, in baskets or as a simple hole in the wall with freestanding grate.

A lot of people take plaster off chimney breasts to make a feature of the brickwork below. But these bricks are generally of inferior quality and were never meant to be exposed. In my experience, people are more likely to re-render and plaster exposed brick chimney breasts when they move in, than vice versa. Exposing brickwork in most houses is not something that will improve the look, saleability or value of your home.

DOORS & ARCHITRAVES
Doors and their surrounds, known as architraves, can be fantastic focal points in a room. To make your living area look grander, replace a standard, 2m high, 762mm wide four-panel particle board door with something taller and wider. Double doors look stunning in the middle of a wall if you have the space, but otherwise a single door with a beautiful architrave will transform a room. Go as high as you can – a 3m door looks really impressive in the right space (you may well need a lintel above it). Reclaimed period doors add character, grandeur and style to the right property, but check that they meet fire regulations.

TELEVISIONS
For many people, the television is the focal point of the room, which seems a shame when there are lots of clever ways to hide it.

DESIGNER REMINDERS

Above: An original stone doorway grabs your attention in this period property. **Below right:** Fireplaces are still very popular focal points. **Opposite:** A sliding panel hides the television when not in use.

Anyone old enough to have seen *Dynasty* or *Dallas* in the 1980s will recall various safes hidden in the wall behind pictures, and you can do exactly the same with a television. Recess it deep into a hole in the wall on motorised arms, hidden by a mirror or picture on parliament hinges, with shelves for DVDs and the remote control behind. Or build a bookcase and hide the television behind an integral door. To make the opening flush, cut the spines to about an inch deep and stick them on – it has to look believable, so choose books of different widths and colours. For bedrooms, you can buy an LCD flat-screen television that rises up out of a panel at the foot of the bed.

Above: Whether these folding doors are open or closed there is always a view of the garden, creating an illusion of space. **Opposite:** A view down a corridor at Dyrham Park with the painting 'A View Down a Corridor' by Samuel van Hoogstraeten in the background.

Garden Views

The view of wrought-iron railings through French doors in upper floors is tremendously effective. It doesn't actually give extra space, but seeing an interesting detail that bit further away brings the outside in. It's a perfect example of how effective a sight line can be at creating the illusion of space. In a property, incorporate as many good vistas as you can – even 'borrowed' ones from nearby green spaces or roof tops. Suddenly coming across a view of a corner of a roof garden or verandah packed with window boxes brings an interesting interplay of indoors and outdoors. Site a chair there so you can sit and enjoy the view, and think about increasing your pleasure in it by laying a complementary coloured or textured floor, or using bold curtains or painted shutters to frame it.

Design your garden, patio space or window boxes to be seen from indoors as well as outdoors – the weather in this country is so unpredictable you can't use the garden as much as you'd like, but you can benefit from seeing it through the kitchen door.

A big patch of lawn surrounded by dishevelled borders is never a good selling point. You can do amazing things with some repeat planting, paving and a good sense of geometry. Try to stick to only a few different colours of flowers – especially in a small space. Concentrate on the structure of the garden. Long straight lines are usually a mistake, dividing a garden into boring blocks. Instead, create horizontal interest by staggering pathways in bold lateral shapes or curving them snakelike down the garden. Then add vertical features – an arch, a tree – at strategic points.

Trompe L'oeil

These optical illusions temporarily 'trick the eye' into believing a two-dimensional image is three-dimensional reality, and are often used to make a space seem bigger. Specialist decorators can paint murals or lay tiles to create false doors or windows with views, walls with fake bricks or stonework, and ceilings to give vistas of the sky. Outside, you can 'borrow' views, by framing a distant building or green space with planting. Trompe l'oeil creates an illusion that makes the viewer suspend disbelief. Ten seconds later, they cotton on it's a trick but hopefully will be amused enough to think, how clever!

THAT LITTLE BIT EXTRA...

Create a sight line into your back garden from your front hallway using light. Uplight a path or a few feature plants in the garden and connect them so they come on with the hallway lights to create a feeling of extra space in the evening.

Lighting

Lighting makes the most tremendous difference to a room. You can take a basement flat with no windows and make it feel light, bright and welcoming just by using clever artificial lighting. Yet it is also one of the most difficult things to do well. Ideally, you should plan lighting very early in a development, yet until the room is finished with every chair in place and every picture on the walls, you don't know exactly where you want it. It takes a huge leap of imagination to get it right and the earlier you start visualising what you want, the more likely you are to succeed.

Electric lighting is so central to our lives that we forget it hasn't been around for very long at all. Although the rich and fashionable could buy newly invented electric filament lights from the late 1870s, it wasn't until the creation of a national grid in 1926 and its rollout during the 1930s that electricity became cheaper and more accessible. A pendant overhead and a side lamp on the table gave more useful hours in the day and changed the way ordinary people lived. Today lighting has become more sophisticated, creating exciting visual effects in a room.

Really effective lighting highlights people, areas or furniture you want to focus on, and manipulates how you use a space. It can create changes in mood, shadow and texture and even affect the way you feel about a room. You hardly notice good lighting, whereas bad lighting screams out at you – too bright or too dark, glaring or ineffective. Lighting is something many people struggle with. One of the keys is to try to avoid ever seeing the bulb, so you get the effect without seeing the source of light. That's tricky to achieve, but worth attempting because a well-lit home is a subtle and not that expensive way to add value and increase saleability. People won't quite know why they like your property, but like it they will.

Borrowing Light

Before you redo your lighting, think about ways to steal as much natural light as you can from other sources. Put fanlights over doors, glass panels in doors, or build glazed walls to throw light into a dark central space. In basements or living rooms, pinch light from the floors above through lightwells or sandblasted glass panels in the ceiling, or put in sun tunnels, ducted tunnels with mirrors to bounce light into a room (the shorter the tunnel with fewer bends, the brighter the light). But be aware that this is natural light and you will also need to shut it off, especially in bedrooms (moonlight shining through a sun tunnel can be extremely bright). Shutters, curtains or blinds will do the trick.

Lighting Plan

When you're doing major renovations, plan the lighting as early as you can. If you're redoing the lighting in an existing room, make a scale drawing showing natural light sources and fittings such as fireplaces and doors. Then think hard about how you want to use the space. Will you be reading or watching television, socialising or working there? Is the room used mostly during

DESIGNER REMINDERS

If you're rewiring a property, always take the opportunity to rethink the lighting. It's a good chance to get it spot on.

Fit dimmers in all possible situations, including bathrooms, bedrooms and kitchens. They are not expensive and create fantastic mood effects at the flick of a switch.

You might not think a central pendant light is interesting, but you can buy stunning light fittings that transform a room. If the buyer likes it, they'll be willing to pay extra. If not, replace it with a standard plastic one and take it with you.

Always build in more electrical points than you think you need. If there's a possibility you might want a side light there, put in a socket. It doesn't cost much at the time, but doing it as an afterthought can be horrendously expensive.

Above: Borrowing light via glass bricks and subtle downlighting. **Opposite**: Three sources of lighting – natural light from skylights, downlighters and fun pendant lights in the eating area.

daylight or at night? Where will you sit, and where are the entry points and high traffic areas of the room? Are there any specific artworks or pieces of furniture you want to highlight?

Then you can get down to designing the kind of lighting you want. Think about the level of diffuse background light that will make the space comfortable. Plan accent lighting to create areas of focus and shade; task lighting without glare for close work

areas and reading, and spot lighting for features. Mark the lighting with directional arrows on the plan to create an interplay of darker and lighter areas, with the lighting sources at different heights to give added interest. Then plan where the switches will be – definitely near the door, but perhaps also where you sit and read.

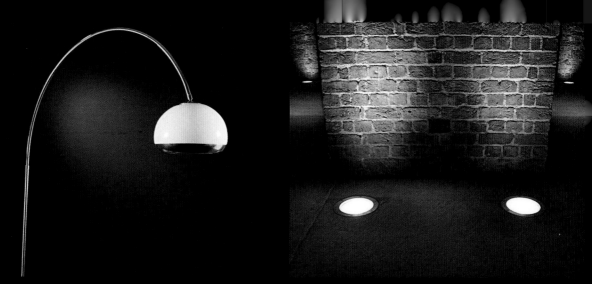

Left: A 1960s Arco floor lamp. **Right**: An old brick interior wall is lit up by spotlights set in a stone floor.

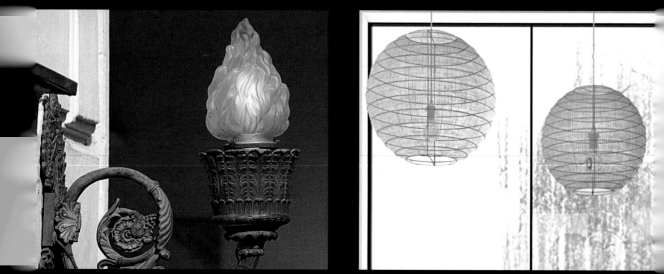

Left: Antique wall lamp with flame-inspired glass shade. **Right**: Paper lanterns for economy background lighting.

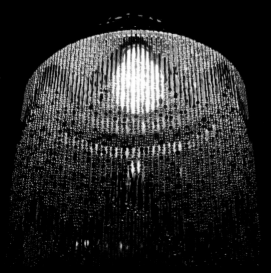

Left: Reproduction pendant with beaded fringe. **Right**: A classic desk lamp provides task lighting.

Left: Glass pendant light for halogen bulbs. **Right**: Modern chrome chandelier for general lighting.

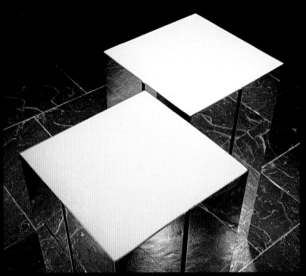

Left: A pair of George Kavacs-designed light box pedestals. **Right**: Two spheres provide atmospheric light.

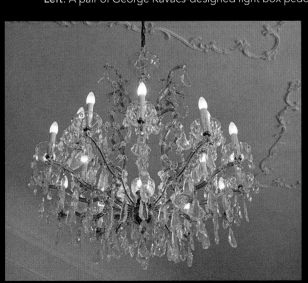

Left: Decorative lighting from an antique chandelier. **Right:** Pewter table lamp and silk shade in Art Nouveau style.

Different Lighting Effects

In any room, there is ambient or background lighting, the level of light from daylight or that traditional single pendant hanging from the centre ceiling. It is flat and dull like a midsummer's day, with no shadows or areas of drama.

Add to it with accent lighting which will bring focus and shade to a space.

The simplest way is to put a lamp on a table, but uplighters, downlighters, spots and track lighting focus on different areas of a room. I think the key is to have light at different heights within a room. You may want to dispense with overhead lights completely and use wall sconces, standard or low-level table lamps instead. I personally would be very wary of using recessed downlighters. Your ceiling is full of holes and you soon find that changing 18 bulbs a week is not a lot of fun. The day of the downlighter has passed, in my opinion. They give a harsh, unflattering light and determine the style of your room or property in a way that a light fitting doesn't. I'd be more tempted to go with spot lighting and a traditional or contemporary central light fitting.

Uplighters are very effective, giving a soft diffuse glow and adding interest at various heights, from the floor or wall sconces. They are second only to candlelight in flattering skin colour, so think about using them in areas where you entertain. Highlight a couple of areas or features in a room. 'Floor washers' are recessed low into a wall to throw diffuse light over a whole floor area, while 'wall washers' highlight a feature wall. Side lights are a great way to give interesting pools of light, especially beside a fireplace or mantelpiece, an easy area to forget. Bookshelves can be backlit or frontlit to give very different effects. It is always a good idea with individual lighting units to fix them into a lighting circuit with a switch by the door. It's handy to use and looks fabulous when you turn them all on in one go.

Task lighting throws bright light on to one specific area. In kitchens you need task lighting for cooking, in living areas for reading, sewing or drawing, in offices for

Above: Tall floor lamps direct the light at the black tiled ceiling; it's then reflected back, providing soft illumination.

Above: This table lamp offers two types of lighting: task over the reading chair and low-level general lighting.
Below: These bookshelves are lit from behind enabling you to find the book you're looking for very easily.

working. It needs to be bright – at least 60 watts – but not so focused you end up with glare or working in your own shadow. Anglepoise lamps are the cheapest solution, though can feel harsh and overbright. For reading and computer work a more diffuse background light is needed to send light from behind on to the book or screen. Spot and picture lights throw directional light on to one surface or feature, but you need to avoid glare, especially off glass. Dedicated picture lights can be positioned below or above: there's more visual drama when they're lit from below but the fitting looks more discreet above the picture.

Above: Traditional lighting in a dream kitchen. **Below:** A splash of coloured light creates a different mood.

Lighting Rooms

KITCHEN

You need bright light in a kitchen, especially around work surfaces, sinks, ovens and hobs. It's a good idea to build in as many integral lights as possible, for example into cooker hoods and under wall cupboard units. Mini-fluorescent strips don't get hot and send a diffuse, warm light on to surfaces below – make sure it is below eye level to avoid glare. Recessed downlights are practical if you have a low ceiling height but have been around a while now and no longer look cutting edge. Directional lighting on tracks or wire is more flexible, or think about hanging two or three small pendant lights to give a diffuse but reasonably bright glow over the whole area. If you have open shelving or glass-fronted display cupboards, make a feature by backlighting them. You can also get a bright but diffuse glow by putting fluorescent strips above wall-mounted units so that light bounces down off the ceiling.

BATHROOM

You need two kinds of lighting in a bathroom: bright focused light near mirrors and a gentle, relaxed light for bathing. Many bathroom cupboards and mirrors now come with integral lighting so all you may need is a dimmer switch for the central light. Fibre optics are practical and safe around water, using neither electricity nor generating heat. They can look striking sunk into flooring and you can fix phased, interchangeable colour versions above a shower to suit your mood. Safety is the primary issue in a bathroom, and all electricity fittings need to be double-insulated and encased to avoid electric shocks, with light switches outside or on a pull cord.

BEDROOMS

Most people settle for an overhead light and a bedside lamp, which is a shame because the bedroom is one lighting zone in which you can go to town. There are stunning bedheads with integral lighting which are a feature in themselves. Remember that the bedroom is a place for relaxation and sleeping, so you don't want to overlight the space or create any glare from thousands of downlights. Instead, go for a layered light look, highlighting alcoves, backlighting sandblasted glass wardrobes or washing light on to a feature wall away from the bed. You need focused task lighting at a dressing table, so ensure that this is on a separate switch. A dimmer switch is crucial for mood lighting, and do make sure that bedside lamps can be switched off separately. For anyone who is gadget mad, you can get a voice-activated light switch so you can tell your lights to switch on or off without getting out of bed.

THAT LITTLE BIT EXTRA...

Light up the insides of built-in wardrobes, closets and cupboards with a tiny sensor, so that when you open the door, the light comes on. It's a simple, low-cost trick which is both practical and luxurious, and makes a home well-considered and pleasant to live in. It also means you'll tend to keep the cupboard doors neatly shut the rest of the time.

Below: Light-diffusing panels on the window, downlights and an adjustable desk lamp for use by the bed.

Design Trickery

Clever lighting tricks enlarge space. The golden rule is the more you can make it look like natural daylight, the more effective it is. Failing that, make the light a feature in itself.

Window light boxes give the illusion of natural light streaming in from outside. Build a window with sandblasted glass into a false wall at the end of a corridor, basement or living room area. In the cavity behind, put a light box plugged into a switched lighting circuit, so bright light shines through into the room. It's hugely effective at creating the illusion of space beyond.

A light source above a drop or suspended ceiling will bring a diffuse, sophisticated light to a living room. The drop ceiling is smaller than the true ceiling, so light shines around the edges of it into the room. It looks very dramatic, especially when the drop ceiling is painted a dark and luxurious colour.

Glass-covered recessed uplighters give gentle illumination set in wooden or stone floors. They look dramatic in corridors or around the edge of large rooms – though be careful the space doesn't end up looking like a museum. You can also put small portholes flush into the side of a wooden staircase, with a light box behind, under the stairs.

A light box on a wall can look like a work of art – hang it centre stage as a feature. It provides light but also draws attention, especially if you have interchangeable colour displays. Set it on a separate dimming control system so you can alter brightness to suit the mood.

Illuminated furniture looks extraordinary – you can get interactive stool/seats which light up in glowing, luminous colours when you sit on them, and switch off when you stand up. To create different moods and set lighting scenes, use a preset dimming control, programmed with a handheld-remote control.

Eco-Friendly Light

Old-fashioned incandescent tungsten bulbs are being voluntarily phased out by manufacturers over the next few years and, by 2011, we'll be using energy-efficient bulbs and other light sources.

Energy-efficient (EE) bulbs, also known as compact fluorescent bulbs, use a fifth of the energy of incandescent bulbs, so are better for the environment and your pocket. They also last longer – around six years. As they are fluorescent, they can take minutes to reach their full capacity and some flicker when used with dimmer switches. They give out a cold, blue-tinged light, and although you can now get 'warm' tones these are less energy efficient. EE bulbs also contain mercury, so need to be recycled carefully.

Fibre-optic lighting emits coloured light along optical fibres. It is cool to the touch, and can safely be used in bathrooms and swimming pools. It is excellent for creating mood – you can now buy fibre optic chandeliers.

Halogen bulbs are less eco-friendly than EE bulbs but 10–15 per cent more efficient and much longer-lasting than incandescent tungsten bulbs. They are very compact in size, and can be used with dimmer switches. They give a light most like daylight, which is cold, crisp and strong.

LEDs (light-emitting diodes) are the most eco-friendly and long-lasting, but are currently only available in low-power versions which don't give out bright light. They are good for accent and mood lighting, for garden lighting, and also in children's bedrooms because they emit hardly any heat and come in colours like red and blue.

Above: General lighting from a variety of sources, selected for its look as well as the quality of light it provides.
Below left: Cubes of light double up as stools. **Below right:** Sophisticated kitchen with floating ceiling panel.

Above: A dramatic basement staircase is lit using external stainless steel recessed step lights. The grasses are uplit by fibre optics, which have been interspersed between them, casting shadows up the wall.

Outdoor Lighting

If you have a kitchen extension or conservatory at the back of a property, the garden will be in full sight, and it makes sense to light it beautifully so you can enjoy the view day and night. Outdoor lighting is most effective when it highlights something sculpturally. You see many gardens with a string of freestanding bollard lights plonked along pathways. Resist the temptation – it always looks like a woodland trail gone wrong. Instead, think of using focus lighting to pick out a dramatic tree, plant or water feature. Try it out first by clipping strong, battery-powered torches above and below your chosen spots. See how it looks from inside the house, with the lights on. Backlighting – where you throw a light behind a shape – makes the outline glow, while uplighting throws the shape into dramatic relief. Don't choose to highlight too many areas as it will look cluttered. Moonlighting – where a low-wattage light is set in a tree to cast pools of light and shadow below – is extremely effective above a patio or seating area. You feel as if you are sitting in moonlight itself.

Although some areas such as steps or water features should be lit for safety reasons, if people are using the garden at night, it's a mistake to flood the whole area with light. It tends to end up looking like a pub garden. You want patios and terraces where you eat and relax to have subtle washes of light, not glaring beams. Again, lovely lighting is invisible lighting, so hide the bulbs and source of the light and aim for a diffuse glow. Submersible white lights can be put into ponds and pools. Fibre-optic lighting is extremely useful in a garden setting (see Resources). It can be sunk into patios or pathways to give a starry effect, or you can use it around pools, ponds and waterfalls to bounce coloured light off the surface of the water, to give an effect almost like fireworks.

It's dangerous to run garden lights from an internal electricity source. Instead, invest in an outdoor power socket. You can run safe, low-voltage spotlight kits off it, with a cable which you can bury, so can position the lights where you like.

Security Lighting

Security lighting is a great idea, not just to deter burglars but also to provide a welcoming light outside the front door and stop people tripping over in the dark. All too often, security lighting is horribly harsh and intrusive, triggered by a passive infra-red (PIR) sensor to be on for 20 seconds whenever anyone walks past. It's less annoying for neighbours if you situate the sensor inside a gate – always make sure you have a facility to switch it on from inside the house – and with the light above the front door rather than glaring across the street. It's also more environmentally friendly to use a low-wattage unit if you can.

DESIGNER NONSENSE

Don't feel pressurised to have trendy chrome-effect or brass-effect light switches or sockets. Light switches don't have to be a feature and, unless they are really great, should blend into the wall.

Period Overview

Tudor 1485-1649

1 Original Tudor long house.
2 Restored inglenook fireplace for cooking.
3 Beamed ceilings were often painted.
4 Diamond-shaped quarries (glass).
5 Typical 16th-century inglenook fireplace.
6 Different shades of oak in the panelling and furniture.

Stuart 1650–1713

1 Melton Constable Hall, Norfolk, built 1644–70.
2 Dogleg staircase dating from the mid-17th century.
3 Six-panelled oak door, *c.*1650.
4 Brick paviors replaced earth floors in rural areas.
5 & 6 Examples of English, Baroque-style pannelled rooms (dining room furniture is early 19th century).
7 Rococo settee in a William and Mary country house.

1

2

3

4

5

6

7

Georgian 1714–1811

1 Georgian townhouse with classical proportions.
2 Turned sticks and polished mahogany handrail.
3 Fireplace with a broken pediment.
4 Uncluttered Georgian sitting room with shutters.
5 An authentic colour for elegant panelling.
6 Stairs had pride of place from around the 1720s.
7 Stone floors were often used in this period.

Regency 1812–1837

1 Bow-fronted windows in a late-Georgian terrace.
2 Fanlights featured in early 19th century properties.
3 A marble fireplace was considered prestigious.
4 Regency-style staircase with plain square sticks.
5 Varnished shutters in a Regency villa.
6 Opulent, colourful room with extravagant drapes.

1

2

4

5

3

6

Victorian 1839–1901

1 Victorian terraced houses came in many forms.
2 *Trompe l'oeil* (used in 18th and 19th century).
3 Wallpaper was not uncommon on the ceiling.
4 Typical Victorian, cast-iron, tiled fireplace.
5 Highly decorated and heavily draped door.
6 Victorian taste demanded a spectacular stairway.
7 Rich colour and pattern dominate Victorian style.

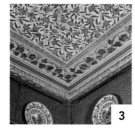

Arts and Crafts 1870–1910

1 The Gamble House (1908), California, USA.
2 Stained glass doors in hallway.
3 Beaten copper fireplace made in 1904.
4 Cottage-style front door of Arts and Crafts house.
5 Natural vegetable dye colours are true to type.
6 Staircase in a grand Arts and Crafts house.

1

2

3

4

5

6

Art Nouveau 1890–1914

1 Gothic-style houses designed by John Douglas.
2 Lincrusta wallpaper, Art Nouveau style.
3 Late 19th-century strong coloured tiles.
4 Art Nouveau stained glass patterns.
5 The Voysey Room in the Geffrye Museum, London.
6 The newel post was a major feature of staircases.

Edwardian 1901–1914

1 Front entrances, similar to Victorian precursors.
2 Chimneypiece with a classical feel.
3 Edwardian terrace with casement windows.
4 Brick fireplace in an Edwardian-style sitting room.
5 Central heating radiator in a grander home.
6 Sticks were mass produced at this time.

1

2

3

4

5

6

Art Deco 1925–1939

1 Fine example of an 1930s Art Deco house.
2 Chain-hung pendant light with geometric design.
3 Couch made in New York in the 1930s.
4 Art Deco apartments with metal windows.
5 Mid-1930s living room with tiled fireplace.
6 Mirrored glass gives a classic Art Deco effect.

Mock Tudor 1930s onwards

1 Familiar semi-detached mock-Tudor houses.
2 Tiled fireplace from around 1930.
3 Plain dogleg staircase with an oak handrail.
4 1930s-style apartment with gramophone.
5 Polished floorboards in a simple living room.
6 Oak parquet flooring was popular at this time.
7 Original light fittings, picture rail and cornice.

1

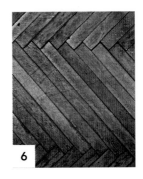

2

3

4

5

6

7

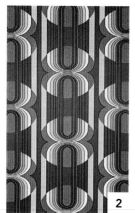

Post War 1945–1960s

1 Larger semi-detached suburban house.
2 Wallpaper design from the late 1960s.
3 Plain windows in a 1960s house.
4 Patterned wallpaper from the 1950s.
5 Stylish 1960s sitting room.
6 Solid fuel stove set in a simple tiled surround.

1970s onwards –
Contemporary Style

1 Flat-roofed house with large picture windows.
2 Open-tread staircase with steel balusters.
3 Plain, minimalist interior.
4 Gas coal fire in contemporary style.
5 A wall of windows letting light flood in.
6 Barcelona chairs in a modern apartment.

1

2

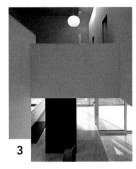

3

4

5

6

Index

Picture credits

KEY

C: Corbis
I: iStockphoto
IPC: IPC+Syndication
NT: National Trust Photo Library
S: Shutterstock
OPG: Octopus Publishing Group
BB: Boundary Bathrooms
CCR: Clements Conservation Rooflights
CSW: Clements Steel Windows
F&B: Farrow & Ball

JCL: John Cullen Lighting
Myspace: Myspace Garden Studios
Sanctuary: Sanctuary Garden Offices
SNKC: Second Nature Kitchen Collection
Splash: Splash Distribution
SS: Sunfold Systems

t top; **b** bottom; **m** middle;
c centre; **l** left; **r** right

2 JCL; 4 Splash; 5 F&B; 6 (l) SNKC; 6 (t r) Evitavonni; 6 (b r) Talisman London; 7 (l) www.lightyourgarden.co.uk 7 (t r) Roger Oates; 7 (b r) CSW; 10 C; 12 I; 13 Back to Front Exterior Design; 14 (t) OPG; 14 (b) C; 15 I; 16 (t l and r, m l, b l and r) I; 16 (m r) S; 17 (t l and r) I; 17 (m l and r; b r) S; 17 (b l) J. Phillimore; 18 S; 19 S; 20 SS; 21 (t l, b l) J. Phillimore; 21 (t r) IPC; 21 (m l and c, b r) I; 21 (m r) S; 22 I; 23 C; 24 (t l, b r) I; 24 (m l and c, b l) S; 24 (t r; m r) Gordon Brown Roofing; 26 J. Phillimore; 27 (t) NT; 27 (b) www.lightyourgarden.co.uk; 28 NT; 30 (b l) I; 31 (t) Camper & Nicholson; 31 (t r) CC Concepts Ltd; 31 (b r) John Strand; 32 SNKC; 33 (t) SS; 33 (b) SNKC; 34 (t l) S; 34 (t r) I; 34 (m l and r, b l) SNKC; 35 (t l and r, m l and r,) SNKC; 35 (b l) S; 35 (b r) Evitavonni; 36 C; 37 (t l) S; 37 (t r; b) IPC; 38 Evitavonni; 39 C; 42–43 SNKC; 44 OPG; 45 IPC; 46–47 IPC; 48 C; 49 NT; 50 NT; 52 S; 53 C; 54 (t) C.P. Hart; 54 (b) C; 55 IPC; 56 (t l; m r) C.P. Hart; 56 (t r) NT; 56 (m l, b l and r) S; 56 (m r) BB; 57 (t l; b r) Evitavonni; 57 (t r) S; 57 (b l) C.P. Hart; 57 (m l) Taylor's Etc; 57 (m r) BB; 58 C; 59 Ambience Bain; 60 C; 61 IPC; 62 (t) Splash; 62 (b) BB63 IPC; 64 Splash; 66 C; 67 NT; 69 IPC; 70 C; 72 (t l, m l, b l) S; 72 (t r, m r) I; 72 (b r) CSW; 73 I; 74 CSW; 75 IPC; 76 (t l) S; 76 (t r, m l and r) I; 76 (b l) M&N Publishing; 76 (b r) CSW; 77 (t r, m r, b l) I; 77 (t l, b r) S; 77 (m l) CCR; 78 I; 79 C; 80–1 C; 83 (t; b l) IPC; 83 (b r) S; 84 IPC; 86 IPC; 87 SS; 88 (t l) Myspace; 88 (t r) Sanctuary; 88 (m l) I; 88 (m r, b l and r) S; 89 (t l) Myspace; 89 (t r, b l) I; 89 (m l and r, b r) S; 90 IPC; 91 I; 92 GlasSpace; 93 C; 94–95 C; 96 (t l and r) London Basement Co Ltd; 96 (b) C; 98 Sanctuary; 99 (t) Myspace; 99 (b) Sanctuary; 100 C; 102 C; 103 (t) Roger Oates; 103 (b) Crucial Trading; 104 (t l) Roger Oates; 104 (t r, b r) Crucial Trading; 104 (m l) S; 104 (m r, b l) I; 105 (t l and r) S; 105 (m l) Dalsouple;105 (m r, b r) I; 105 (b l) Roger Wilde Ltd 106 S; 107 NT; 108 (t and b) C; 109 IPC; 110–113 C; 115 (t l; b l) IPC; 115 (t r) Amtico;115 (b r) Dalsouple;116 C; 119 C; 120 (t l, m r) F&B; 120 (t r) S; 120 (m l) House Couturier;120 (b l) I; 120 (b r) SNKC;121 (t l, b r) S; 121 (t r) I; 121 (m l and r) F&B; 121 (b l) Burton Constable Hall; 122 (t and b) IPC; 123 C; 124 F&B; 125 (t) C; 125 (b) IPC; 126 (t l and r; b r) C; 126 (b l) IPC; 128–129 Sir John Soane's Museum; 130 C; 131 Burton Constable Hall; 132 S; 134 C; 135 (t) IPC; 135 (b) C; 136 (t l and r, m l, b r) S; 136 (t r, b l) I; 136 (m r) Aestus Radiators; 137 (t l and r, m l, b l and r) S; 137 (m r) I; 138 NT; 139 IPC; 140 IPC; 141 (t) C; 141 (b) IPC; 142–143 C; 144 IPC; 145 NT; 146 JCL; 148 IPC; 149 C; 150 (t l) Talisman London; 150 (t r, b l) S; 150 (m l and r, b r) I; 151 (t l and r) S;151 (m l) Talisman London;151 (m r, b l) I;151 (b r) NT; 152 C; 153 (t) IPC; 153 (b) JCL; 154 (t) C; 154 (b) IPC; 155 C; 157 (t, b r) C; 157 (b l) IPC; 158–159 JCL; 160 JCL.

Pages 162–173 OPG, except for: 164 (1) I; 165 (1) S; 166 (1) S; 167 (1) C; 167 (4) M&N Publishing; 168 (1) S; 169 (1) J. Phillimore; 169 (3) S; 170 (1) C; 171 (1–3, 7) M&N Publishing; 172 (1, 6) M&N Publishing; 172 (2,5) I; 172 (3, 4) S; 173 (1–4) S; 173 (5) CSW; 173 (6) I.